"To travel hopefully is a better thing than to arrive,"

Robert Louis Stevenson's 1878 essay entitled "El Dorado".

Acknowledgements

If this book is a success we owe it to those who have made our travels infinitely rewarding, among these in particular Graham Gingles and Jude Stephens in Northern Ireland, Elizabeth Mulder in Den Haag, Eunice Ipinge in Namibia, Yoshiko Shibata, Kobe University in Japan, Glyne Griffith and Librada Pimental in Albany, the Trinidad and Tobago High Commissioner and staff in India, my sister Badura and her husband Victor Pereira, and her family in Australia, and our many friends and colleagues elsewhere too numerous to mention. To my sister Ramona Lisa Mohammed our thanks for her encouragement of this project.

For agreeing to cast a practiced editorial eye on this unorthodox collection of prose and verse we are grateful to Andy Taitt of Barbados. For her curatorial oversight in selecting illustrations and for their infectious enthusiasm for a travel book that features Rex's drawings and paintings, we thank his very supportive and ever faithful gallery owners Nisha Hosein and Sheriff Khan of Soft Box Studios in Port of Spain, Trinidad.

We have benefitted from logistical support from Tennille Fanovich, Angelica Bencosme, Chelsea Seetahal, and Rennie Pierre. Sheriff Khan, Mike Stanley and Owen Bruce provided photographs of canvases and authors. We were reminded of the kindness of strangers that is at the core of this book when during its publication in the summer of 2016, Finn Hamill at the Royal Avenue Belfast Central Library went out of her way to facilitate an urgent request.

For the translation of an idea that lay dormant for many years into a physical reality we are truly appreciative of the painstaking care and creativity of graphic artist Anya Pierre. And to Arif Ali and his team at Hansib Publications, thank you for working with our specific design requests and adding this one to your booklist.

Introduction

Come up and see my etchings...

The title of this book is a pastiche of Robert Louis Stevenson's *Travels with a Donkey* (1879) and Graham Greene's *Travels with my Aunt* (1970), neither reference literal but nonetheless some parallels may be drawn. RLS's book is about his perambulations with a donkey named Modestine through the Cévennes district of France in 1879. Modestine was a very obstinate animal which did not want to go where it was told. This contribution and collusion with the title is with Rex's full permission and support. *My Aunt* became *A Husband*. The double entendre in the indefinite article is deliberate, open to anyone's interpretation.

The book is a journey about friendships and memories, about marriage, companionship and work, an autobiography in prose, verse and drawings, a travelogue, an adventure in style. Rex and I have journeyed as reluctant tourists rather than as voyeurs. Most, but not all of our voyages, have been fitted around work related activities. One of the perks of a fairly successful academic career is the opportunity to see the world through relatively privileged circumstances, always protected by the network and codes that surround university fraternity on visits for the business of education. Immigration authorities seem to have a second sense that sniffs out the academic traveller, and questions about a visit have generally been perfunctory, especially as return tickets establish precise ingress and egress. As a full-time professional painter, Rex has had the flexibility of time to travel with me not only for leisure but to explore his own discipline.

It is autobiographical because it is also a record of a creative and intellectual partnership of over two decades captured through essays, vignettes, poetry, doggerel, drawings and individualized postcards. Some of the verse makes no pretense at poetry but are nonsense rhyme, inscribing in our memory place, event, people and time. As an academic and filmmaker

Patsy's Birthday Card – Goache on paper, 4x6 ins – 2004

my tendency is to record encounters through text and photographs while the visually trained Rex, absorbs emotion and event in line, tone and colour. He generally produces some manner of artwork that is influenced by the places we passed through or those in which we have resided for some time. Because it deals with travels over two decades it is also about a development of styles and perception over this period. My contributions are reflective of history or social attitudes. Rex interprets, sometimes with humour, events and situations with different artistic nuances and mediums.

Memory moves back and forth in this book as it does in real life. Flashback to the beginning in 1994 and our first adventure, or should I say meeting. The slender fair haired Englishman did not really issue the clichéd "Come up and see my etchings sometime", but it was understood by the end of my visit to the painting department of the Edna Manley School for the Visual Arts in Jamaica that I had been encouraged to Rex's studio to look at his work. I had shortly before arrived to take up the Headship of the newly formed Centre for Gender and Development Studies at the University of the West Indies, Kingston, Jamaica. During the period of my doctoral studies in Den Haag, I had attached myself to the atelier of one of the successful Dutch painters of this city, continuing a lifelong and more than amateurish interest in visual arts, even producing an exhibition of drawings and paintings on paper by the time I had submitted the dissertation. In seeking out the Edna Manley art school, I had in mind to continue my artistic development alongside the disciplinary academic demands of the new post. I did go to see his etchings in the coming weeks. The studio turned out to be a fairly large garage full of canvases and drawings. Fresh from a five-year immersion in the contemporary style of the Dutch painters I related to its abstraction and whimsy, and went to the exhibition he had by the following month at Grosvenor Gallery, Manor Park, with the intention of buying a single piece. By the following year we were married and I acquired the whole oeuvre.

The pieces contained here are episodic rather than sequential although there is some evidence of a chronology, because the journeys are for the most part academic and work related, some overlapping different trips to the same site. The drawings were selected from several hundreds in Rex's many portfolios and because of his style are not necessarily literal executions of the societies or even the event that it illustrates. They however signal our emotions or feelings about the particular place or event. Some are elaborations done on photographs generally taken by myself transmitted onto paper that Rex worked over with gouache and ink. There are a few canvases selected, but the majority are works on paper. Rex has ingrained the habit of sending postcards back home to the neighbours and converted this into writing postcards back to ourselves, so the postcards contained drawings, stamps and an image of the place we visited. Some of these are included as illustrations.

It is regretted that only part of these travels are contained in this book, as we also visited and made friends in most of the Caribbean territories including Cayman Islands, Bahamas, St Kitts-Nevis, St Lucia, Belize, The Dominican Republic, San Andreas in Colombia, Guyana and Suriname along with some other non-Caribbean societies, but perhaps that is the second volume to come. Travel used to be viewed in earlier decades as educational or exciting. Now it is greeted with fear and trepidation, the long security lines and the possibility of terrorism. Yet our entire lives have been enriched by travel, taken out of the comfort zones of home and too familiar

Flying Over Jamaica – Mixed Media – 9x12 inches – 2007

culture. This peripatetic lifestyle has led us to settle in more than one place, and we commute as much as possible between Trinidad and the Antrim coast of Northern Ireland every year enjoying the extremes of climate and people. We are, like many others, very much products of the modern condition of being, always transitory migrants, not quite settled in any one place, and wary of the boundaries of nation, class, ethnicity or gender that attempt to define our lives. Like many others, we leave a little of our souls in each place we have visited or lived in for a while, and we take some of theirs with us, always adding to the imaginary landscapes that constantly fuel our creativity and *joie de vivre*.

June 30th 2016

Mexico

Merida, Mexico

Amor in
a hot climate

Merida was warm at the end of May 1994. To be honest, a little more than warm, about 40 degrees in the shade. It was our first trip together, me to attend a Caribbean Studies Association Conference, Rex to begin a tradition of accompanying me on conferences and research trips as companion, guide, map reader, locator of best places to find refreshing drinks of a more tippling variety, reasonable restaurants and "carry your bags Madam". A good division of labour.

Whether it was the heat or the newness of each other's company, we ventured out of doors very little during the day. We went to conference events – and quickly understood why the Spanish invented the concept of afternoon siesta, when to simply lift a finger brought a sprinkle of sweat gems to one's forehead.

We sampled Mexican breakfasts for sure and learned to love queso (cheese) and refried beans. Rex bought me a straw hat, with a woven band that I have kept to this day, and a little bunch of painted straw flowers, also still in my possession.

This first trip also started the habits that would characterize all our travels – to explore the aesthetic sensibility of a space, its food, music and art, and appreciate its colloquialism. This left each place engraved in our memory to be reproduced either during the trip or later in text or drawings. Some countries we were to visit once only, some many times over, and each journey produced another shared memory to mark time between us.

Merida became an unfinished project of discovery, this time without Rex. Twenty years later, in 2014, I would return for another CSA conference, and completed the pilgrimage we did not take in 1994.

Merida Memory – Ink on paper – 9x7 ins – 2003

We have never been good at handling crowds or excessive noise. Nor are we intrepid travellers willing to undergo privations, heat, stormy weather or undue exertion. An image remains vividly with us of a stiflingly overfilled bus of delegates to the Association of Caribbean Historians conference in Martinique in 1997. We were setting out on a field trip on the final day, the first port of call the site of Mont Pelee's historical eruption in the village of St. Pierre. Above the overheated academic buzz before we actually took off, there was another eruption, "LET ME OFF THE BUS, LET ME OFF THE BUS". Rex's British voice, high pitched with claustrophobia, created immediate silence.

He was in the centre aisle in a pull out seat lower than those beside him and could not see out the windows. The driver knew a cry for help when he heard it. Rows of people had to file out to let us off. Bridget Brereton, Professor in History and stalwart of the Association, has called it a never to be forgotten moment in the Association's annals.

In 1994 in Merida, we had not gone on the planned outings, one of which was a trip to the remnants of Chichen Itza, the largest of the ancient Mayan cities. A primary reason to visit Mexico was the value of Mayan history in my work on Caribbean visual iconography.

In 2014 I returned, without Rex. Twenty years later, he was less sprightly and not very enthusiastic about spending days away from his studio in Maracas Valley. It was a long trip from Merida and the sky was a heavy gray. The air-conditioned bus was just comfortably filled. By the time we got to Chichen Itza, the clouds burst. We walked around in disposable transparent pink and blue raincoats like visitors from another planet. It continued to rain and rain all through the guided tour, the faded yellow-brown brick walls still exuding majesty despite an overcast sky that cast no moving shadows.

Merida Colours – Gouache on paper – 6x4 ins – 2004

The Authors in Merida, 1994

The lush grassy expanses between the Temple of Warriors and the ball court squelched as our unsuitable footwear got soggier and soggier. But the magnificence and resourcefulness of civilizations before us is always moving, knowing that few of our grandiose buildings today will survive the terrors of modern warfare, as these at Chichen Itza have managed since 600 AD.

As we mopped up what we could of half drenched clothes and bags, I thought to myself that the Mayan gods were probably laughing down on us getting their Mexican revenge (of another kind), on the busloads of tourists who had stomped all over their hallowed ground. It was just as well that Rex, the ever-reluctant tourist, had not been there.

December, 2015

Jamaica

The Fisherman of Flagaman and tales of a treasured beach

Armed with black scandal (plastic) bag and cutlass in hand, crouching on the sands of Great Bay in predatory pose, Arkwright burrows after the retreating crab. Widening the crab hole by fistfuls of sand, deeper until, no match for the man, the crab loses legs and claws, and the struggle for life. Another crab bites the sand as it joins the rest, legless and harmless in the scandal bag, linking up with the food chain as bait to lure fish for Arkwright's supper.

Arkwright's technique always draws the onlooker passing the time on this relatively deserted beach. At a glance Arkwright can tell which holes to dig into, the size of the crab and whether it is at home. The largest crabs signposted the biggest holes during the night, their passages to and fro for food a delicate web of patterns on the sand.

Our first day at the seaside, Rex came back from a treasure jaunt for sea shells and told me of this strange man digging crabs to go fishing. Yesterday evening, we spied Arkwright and his scandal bag and cutlass lower down the beach. Early this morning, the sun still low on the south coast Jamaican horizon, I ventured down the beach. There was Arkwright, evoking the comparison with Miss Marianne, all day, all night, down by the seaside she sifting sand. Or the naughty Caribbean version, down by the seaside catching man.

There are no men on this beach to catch. Even the fish seem disinclined to be caught although these are waters teeming with life. For the past five years since we'd met, Rex and I had run away to our resting place from work, Great Bay, a little fishing village at the end of the road, four hours drive from Kingston. If you squint gently in the noonday sun at Great Bay on the left and Treasure Beach far distant to the right, you might think they were parts of

The Intuitives - Ink on paper - 9x12 ins - 2005

Jamaica that time had forgotten. The days run into each other with an assuring monotony. The waves wash sonorously on the front of Pelican Reach, the aptly named rambling cottage on the beach that we rent each time. From the verandah you can see the pelicans perched on docked pirogues diving and plunging after prey. At times the beach is heavy with anger, the waves lashing out at the sand and beating a hasty retreat. Now and then you hear the sound of Justin and Rowena, the housekeeper Angie's children, playing in the backyard, or little boys splashing about like dolphins in the water.

The blue of this sea is not translucent aquamarine like Negril or Montego Bay. It is as changeable as a summer's day on the Antrim coast of Northern Ireland. Prussian blue in mid-morning, with a ribbon of lilac marking the horizon, and a white frothy lace, the shore. By midday it is a thousand pieces of broken glass glinting in the sun. A sea where families come to bathe on weekends and public holidays, amply endowed women wearing brassieres and panties underneath and T-shirts over their bathing suits, and plastic shower caps over their curlered hair. Parents shouting at children not to go too far into the water. Men tossing back Red Stripe beer. Boys playing football on the beach. Every now and then a whitey couple comes along, with Rex, a whitey, always ready to compare how much more evenly tanned he is than these Johnny come lately beachcombers.

Rex ventures out with his fishing line carefully wrapped around the bleach bottle, throwing another line to me, I'm off to bring back the bacon. For five years I've waited for fish to fry and never seen one, he says he throws them back in, I say that he never caught any. He says it's not the catching that's important it's the doing, the patience, the solitude, the quiet waiting for the fish to bite, looking at the colours of the sea and sky, tasting the wind on your face blowing away at your olde straw hat. I envy him the capacity to patiently watch time go by. To sit and look and listen rather than to do all the time. He sees the colours that I don't, he can hear the sound of the wind, he knows what time the john crows come in to roost on the tall pine trees in the garden, he enjoys the rhythm of the day. A painter, perhaps he understands the need to let the brain lie fallow to absorb and implant the colours and textures.

I arrive at these leisurely expeditions with a bagful of textbooks, novels, computer, camera, box of paints and paper. I generally leave feeling that I have caught up with my creative projects, the ones I can never seem to find time to do in Kingston. There are no televisions or telephones here, only the two year old Rowena's toy "circular" (cellular) phone, which one of the numerous goats who wander about the grass seemed to have made a delightful morsel of. Every now and then you hear the goat's stomach bleating out a musical grumble.

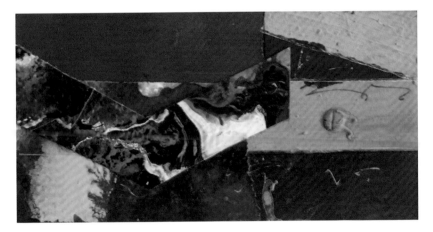

Seascape – Acrylic and collage on paper – 3x6 ins – 2013

This is not true actually, my flight of fancy. Rowena does still have her toy "circular", but this fictional morsel was influenced by a story Angie told us. Angie regaled us on each visit with the goings on of her neighbours, none of whom we actually knew, in tall tales of a magical realism bent. This time it was a Christmas story, the season of great cheer having just passed. According to her, people in a nearby village (in Great Bay itself, needless to say, nobody is dishonest) complained for years that they could be sure of getting their bills in the post, but not cards or letters with money from relatives from 'foreign'. They complaining for years to the post mistress who say she sorry, but that is all she getting and that their relatives not sending them anything. Lacking piped water, many houses had outdoor water closets. One day a man using the P.O. asked the post mistress to use her outdoor facility. Sitting, he could hear coming from the pit a plaintive "Silent night, holy night, All is calm, all is bright". Surely a strange place for a caroller to dwell, and he dismissed the thought. Then a mentally disadvantaged fellow, also hearing the strains of silent night when making use of the postmistress's facilities, rushed out shouting, "Somebody trying to obeah me b...... Dem trying to silence me". Off in the head, maybe, but he made such ruckus in the days after, that the police were called in to investigate. Then all the dirty correspondence was washed in the public – for years the post mistress had been helping herself liberally to the money and cheques sent in the Christmas cards and letters, and discarding the evidence in her WC out back. People's lives had been affected by her mishandling. One girl, every week getting letter and money from her baby father up in the cold, didn't even get so much as a Christmas card from him. She spend a very unhappy Christmas thinking he finish with her if he couldn't even write her and his little baby son. Maybe it was he who sent the silent night musical card. The postmistress was dismissed. Poetic justice, somehow, that a Christmas carol card would give her away, the spirit of Christmas clearly working in strange and mysterious ways.

Angie is a natural born story teller. She doesn't read a book or a newspaper, but she has an ear for the detail of village life. The stories come out easily, like a passing observation, giving the distinct feeling that she is relating an incident that happened up the road a few days ago. She can be sparked by a chance comment about someone you catch sight of on the beach, or meet up in the little sparsely stocked grocery at the end of the road. Each story seems more improbably true than the last. We saw a youngish Rasta man one day, locks yellowing from the seaside sun and saltwater, looking like his clothes could use a

Market Square – Gouache on paper – 14x20 ins – 2001

good wash and iron, walking the beach, throwing the garbage into the water, only for the tide to wash it up again. His head not wrapped round too tight perhaps! Early one morning, I saw him walking along the shore, Red Stripe beer in hand. Too early for Red Stripe, the sun not ready for legitimate cooling down yet. Yesterday, we saw him from a distance, leaning against the shaky blue gate which fenced Pelican Reach. Our response was typical urban fear and distrust - he might be wanting to steal something. In Great Bay it was still possible to do the unbelievable, not lock doors all day, leave the house open and go for a swim. It is a luxury and a right one treasures, perhaps more than the sea itself. We are always afraid that something is going to force us into being watchful, distrustful, tense with strangers, as urban life does. So we asked Angie about him.

Oh, Angie said, he harmless, he just wanted some water from the garden tap to drink. She went on to tell his story. A few years ago, his father died leaving him a nice little bit of property – house and land – in the village. But he was already a drinker and smoker and he sold his house and land, to the man in the adjoining property, for a big brown paper bag full of money. He came to the bar, she said, with a brown paper bag full of money. For two weeks he was never sober, buying for himself and everyone day and night. At the end of the two weeks the brown paper bag of money was finished. Now he has nowhere to sleep, rests his head anywhere he falls down at night, sleeping in the boats on the shore on a cool night, does a bit of manual work for people and drinks out his earnings by the next day.

Thankfully there are not too many stories of wasted youth in Great Bay. The village has retained its charm even after all these years. But each year another little bit of 'kulcha' creeps in. One year it was the thatched bar where the fishing boats come in. To attract clients the bar owner started to blast taped music so loud that if you lie on the sand it quickens under you. Next year, an entrepreneuring rastaman built a shack near to the entrance of Pelican Reach, running a trade in soft drinks and maybe other soft substances for beach visitors – the ambiance of the beachfront invaded just a little bit more.

But all of nature cannot be so easily denuded. On the last day before we left on one visit I spied Arkwright on the beach with a foreign youngster who, fascinated by his technique, was trying to emulate him. I wandered over again to check out the armless crabs he was chucking into the scandal bag. Friendly as ever, the crab business slower today, Arkwright ask if I was from foreign, and I said yes, Trinidad, to which he replied that they have pretty girls there, obviously not including present company in the category - time and tide waiting for no

Intuitive Painters Plus Dog – Gouache on paper – 6x9 ins – 2005

woman. So I say yes but they have pretty girls everywhere in the world, in any event I living in Kingston. He ask when we going back to Kingston. I replied with some reluctance in my voice, the next day. People in town always in a hurry he said. Kingston (or "Kill some" as he referred to it) is a dangerous place. You can't walk about free as you want in the night there. He lives on Flagaman Hill, a few miles from Great Bay. He walks down to the sea, catches his crab and his few fishes, walks back up the hill, night could meet day and he have no worries walking about.

As we reached the Spanish Town roundabout and start the urban crawl into Kingston I remember my last sight of Arkwright, standing on the verge of the rocks, throwing out his fishing line, waiting patiently for a tug, feeling only the bite of the breeze against his skin. I think about Arkwright and the crab antics. Here in front of us are tyre tracks, fumes, rusty zinc fences, the bold face empty stares of people scurrying to and fro. Like the crabs, they run back into dark holes; unlike the crabs they leave no intricate patterns on the surrounding landscape. Or none that I could see.

January, 1999

Jamaica

Mi dawta mi dawta

Gwen standing quiet quiet in de front porch as Jessica come in from work. Blood red hibiscus petals and butchered purple bougainvillea making a rough mat on the tiled floor. Gwen have the kitchen knife in she hand, the sharp sharp one she does use to cut up goat meat and clean the red snapper that Jessica buy from Papine market.

"What happened here, Gwen? Someone come in, somebody try to attack you?" Jessica standing there, looking around her house now in shreds, curtains hanging like loose bandages on twisted rails. Lime green pools of Squeezy splashed about on the cedar floor, a trail of broken glass from room to room.

Gwen like she not even there, eyes dull like burnt out coals. Her mouth like a Salvador Dali clock rim.

She had come to the house as a helper two years ago. Jessica used to leave notes for Gwen to do the chores and realize one evening, when she find half the meal unprepared, and a scrawl, *Mis Jes de bean am bad*, that Gwen could barely read or write. But Gwen was honest and kind and hardworking, a woman of forty-two who look fifty-nine. Jessica liked how Gwen would make her cocoa tea with fresh mint from the garden. She massage Jessica head with olive oil and vetiver for an hour one morning and the headache she had just gone away.

She like working for people who appreciate her, not the kind that shovel work on she back like she still some slave in a canefield. She prefer people from away who had manners and brought-upsy. Jessica was from foreign, not from Jamaica. Mis Jes treat her real good.

For two years now, Monday to Friday, Gwen cross a bumpy track from

34

Mi Dawta, Mi Dawta – Ink on paper – 11x14 ins – 1995

her galvanize hut to the nearest bus stop on Irish Town hill. Then she take the maxi-van down to Halfway Tree, standing room only this hour of the morning, the pusher shouting "Smaal up yuhself, smaal up yuhself," as he shove another body into the back, then a next overcrowded 'smaal up yuhself' bus up to Harringdale Crescent. The bus don't even stop in front of Jessica house. She have to get out at Liguanea and then a five minute walk in the morning sun before she get to the front door. She raise three children this way, working in people house since she turn thirteen. The children dem father never last. The first two stay around long enough to see them pickney born, two boys Jojo and Tobias. She glad to see the back of number one. He use to 'buse her. The second child father had religion but that never stop him from leaving. She manage to get the two son away from trouble early by sending them to live with a relation in de Bronx that she never visit sheself. She eh hear from them lately, but as far as she know they living and she feel she do her duty by them. Babylon bullets na get time to gun them down in Tivoli Gardens.

The last child father, before she tie she belly, was Bobsieboy. He stay longer than the rest. Maybe that is why Mavis come out so good. She make Mavis go to school and stay far away from boys. Mavis Petersfield, primary school pupil teacher now, boarding by respectable Missis Kent in Newtown, wearing white blouse and bright blue pleated skirt and black close up shoes everyday, not like Gwen who still wearing washout *ganzi* and slippers. Gwen talking to sheself proudly as she scrub another pot to cook the rice and peas for Jessica and Cyrus dinner. She thinking, happy while she turning the pot. Mavis Petersfield, maybe school mistress in Campion college. Mavis, her dawta who would keep her company in old age. Mavis visit her every other Sunday with cake and sometimes chicken and chips from KFC. Gwen had manage to get Mavis away from the Don in the village two years ago the day after he cut up Mavis hand with a penknife because she wouldn't go with him. Gwen send Mavis to live uptown so her dawta could be safe.

The two policeman come early that morning. Gwen still asleep, dreaming of reading the bible one day when Mavis find the time to teach her. She didn't cry when they show her Mavis blouse and skirt and ask if she could recognize it. She take it from them quiet quiet. "Like somebody crack a bottle of Red Label wine all over the chile clothes", she say as if talking to sheself. Gwen looking over the clothes like Mavis inside it, the white blouse dirty red and the blue skirt turn mauve in some place. "Mavis uniform need washing" she mumble quietly. She tell them they must leave it with her.

She push the wet clothes into the bag she take to work and rouse sheself up after the policemen gone. She had to get to Jessica house to finish the scrubbing she left yesterday. She took the two bus as usual and find her way to the house in Harringdale Crescent. She walk into the kitchen. Then she pick up the knife and she went to work.

June, 2015

36

Deluge – Acrylic on paper – 12x9 ins – 2010

Kingstown, Jamaica

Passa Passa night
in downtown Kingston

Bodies shake and jump and quiver
Footsteps lined up in a row
Man to one side, women let go,
Moving in time,
One heart beat with the other.

Sensual synchrony on a busy busy road
Cameras light up, capturing the mood
Them smoking spliff
Better pull over they hood.

Two young men absorbing the sight
Fiction blurs in subdued morning light
Rex and Michael checking out the scene
Reference points are not the landscape
But what lies in between
Fran and Hebe in time with the rhythm
The natives look on
And try to get with them
The pavement rocking
The buses too close
But nobody stopping
Nobody want to go home
Midnight on the sidewalk of good and evil
There's really no choice
Let dawn take the devil.

July, 2009

Passa Passa Night – Ink on paper – 5x22 ins – 1991

Trinidad

Mayaro, Trinidad

Uneventful days
in Mayaro

Mayaro village and beach was a place for which I had fond childhood memories of summer vacation holidays with my parents. On a visit from Jamaica one year, I wanted to take Rex to experience this part of Trinidad. The Mayaro coastline on the east Atlantic seaboard of Trinidad was never a beach for swimming carelessly. There were no restrictions however against wading along the water's edge and collecting *chip chip* (sea shells) by the bucket – which my mother would later curry – or splish splashing about in one of the shallow rivulets which ran into the sea, and building sandcastles like those children in Enid Blyton books did when they went to the seaside.

I had not been down to Mayaro for years. I suppose in the way of all flesh I was seduced into the urban Trinidadian ideas of the popular beach spots – Maracas on a Sunday morning for shark and bake, down the islands at Monos at my sister Linda's time shared beach cottage or ruddy scenic Toco if one wanted more high strung rock-filled adventure. The drive to Mayaro from the northern side of the island is quintessential tropical scenery, especially when you arrive at the Manzanilla stretch of coastline along the east coast with coconut trees lining the roadside and the wild heliconia like sparks of orange fire among the greenery.

The village of Mayaro was far more ordered and impressive than I recalled, but then, my childhood visits predated the major expansion of oil drilling in the adjacent district of Guayaguayare. The police station was located across the road from the hospital; there was a good weekend market, well-stocked pharmacy and grocery, and cooking gas available on a Sunday morning when the gas inevitably ran out. The house we stayed in was not

Mayaro Blues – Mixed Media – 8x12 ins – 2008

luxurious by any means but there was water and electricity, a well-equipped kitchen, plenty of rooms to spread sand around in, and more than enough beds. It did not even bother to have a name like some of the more impressively kept seaside properties such as "Why Worry" and "Sound of the Sea". It was prime real estate though. A covered front porch and wrapped around balcony overlooked the beach. For miles down the coast, on each direction, one could sit all day on the veranda, the outlines of the two headlands spanning the reach of vision to the right and left, the horizon thirty miles in front, a gash of deep blue containing a shifting emerald sea. Sit there with an early morning cup of tea followed by breakfast and another cup of coffee, followed by lunch, not even touching the water, taking part in the silent movie which plays out on the beach from dawn to dusk against the never ending orchestra of the waves.

Even before the two or three toned lifeguards in faded yellow T-shirts and rustic red shorts come out to plant their windblown red and yellow flags, the beach is alive. An old woman fully clothed with her head tie firmly wrapped, comes out with a little white pail and proceeds to bathe herself in the sea – dipping the pail and pouring it over her head onto her back, lifting her skirt and drenching her legs. A few purposeful walkers continue their morning constitutional, dogs running gaily alongside, dipping into the water now and then to cool off, bothering the little fishes doing their little fishy swim.

The lifeguards on Mayaro are impressive, not because they display Baywatch physiques and buns of steel, but because they carry out their job efficiently, with courtesy and good humour. The painted sign on the beachfront warns bathers to bathe only between the red and yellow flags. Each day the lifeguards place the red and yellow flags in short distance from each other at two points on the beach and they concentrate all bathers at this point, monitoring their waywardness in the water if necessary. One or two of the lifeguards patrol the beach and urge the wayward beachgoers to bathe only between the stipulated areas. One day we were all sand bathing in quite shallow waters in front of our house and the lifeguard passed by. "It safe to bathe here?" my brother Dicky queried, concerned for his little girls Danielle and Nadia. "Only if you stay on the ground," the lifeguard replied. His meaning and message was quite clear to us.

If the fishermen have been out to throw the nets the night before, then the choreography of pulling in the *seine* (nets) begins on the beach. Two rows of men, heaving and towing in synchronized unison, moving closer and closer together, the morning sun boring into their skins while the sharp twang of the ropes scar their calloused hands. The catch is not a good one, many little fishes in the midst of the seaweed and flotsam. The fishermen must work quickly to get the best of their catch while too many people have gathered to scavenge the net for what they could get freely. Apparently the fishing is not good here any more; only one pirogue is visible on the shore of a once thriving fishing village.

The day passes on – amateur fishermen stand mid-thigh in the water in the solitary game of casting and recasting the fishing line secured around a bleach bottle. Rex looks on enviously, wishing he had brought his favourite bleach bottle fishing tackle. But he consoled himself to look on contentedly like me from the distance, at the fishermen and at the children who feel no heat in the midday sun. Their fingers and toes wrinkling from being submerged in water, they steadfastly refuse to leave the shore – *chip chip* gatherers who are made to throw back their treasure at the end of the day.

Then the evening cast arrives. A young well built torso seen from this distance. Three or four young boys are being taught karate or judo by their *sensei* on the beach. What better place to hold an open-air gym, the sand to cushion the falls, the breeze to blow away sweat and exertion. This budding Ato Boldan races his young counterparts up and down the beach while less energetic groups of men play wind ball cricket lower down the shore, the outfielders knee deep in the rising tide.

We go out for our evening constitutional. Scavengers of another sort, looking for driftwood, which has weathered into imagined shapes. Examining the transparent purples and pinks of the jellyfish, multi-coloured creatures washed up by the tide. A quick dip in the water and back to our balcony to watch the sun go down fading slowly and gently, reluctantly leaving the lanky coconut trees, taking away the shadows from the sand, transforming the sea into a darker mysterious blue green deep. The lifeguards arrive in their beat up Red Cross van and drive along the beach, removing the red and yellow flags they had planted in the morning, a daily reminder of danger in the midst of this idyllic Edwin Hingwan watercolour.

July, 1996

Mayaro Sunset – Gouache on paper – 4x6 ins – 2010

Trinidad

Cricket watching and other voyeuristic sports

(for Ayoob Mohammed)

My father and uncle used to play against a team called Yorkshire in the little village of Cunjal in south Trinidad in the early sixties. I remember going to see a 'fete match' one Sunday afternoon, with the entire family. The host team generally provided refreshments for the visitors. It was not just a tea break. My father regular returned from a cricketing afternoon out the worse for drink.

As a spectator, the cricket grounds in sunny green, its central brown rectangular pitch, the players scattered irregularly throughout the field, had absolutely no meaning to me other than the obvious: they were waiting to field or catch the ball depending on where the batsman sent it. They looked resplendently clean and smart against the rich pasture, elegant moving white stick figures with black bobbing heads in the distance. While I had no fine appreciation of field positions like silly mid on and silly mid off or the bowling tactics of spin bowling or googly, my eyes caught the exquisiteness of the rural setting from an ordered distance, uncrowded wooden houses and reddish discoloured galvanized roofs visible through the trees, overgrown bushes edging the field, a flowering shrub here or there relieving shades of green. "A lovely day for cricket" as the popular Trinidadian calypso said, "Blue skies and gentle breeze," but in my calypso take, one village group was playing against another village team, not England playing the West Indies.

Like all the players, my father dressed for this role as Sunday afternoon cricket player. He wore his white serge trousers, white "watchekongs' with socks, white long sleeved cotton shirt, crisply starched and ironed, and a knitted waistcoat with red and black stripes around the hips, just like the ones worn by the players in the photographs of the English and West Indies teams. Although I did not then appreciate the finer points of the game, one could not grow up in the West Indies and be unmindful of the seriousness with which these young men and the various cricket clubs took the sport. It was not just about dressing up and catching up with the curves of a ball on the lawn. The trappings of the cricket match, the chunks of silence while the game was being played, the rules of sportsmanship, the slow pace of each game interrupted by water breaks, the afternoon revelry and ribbing after, was a very anglicized tradition, inherited by all who had had a long spell of British rule. One accepted this unquestioningly, as we did another tradition of fundraising school bazaars with its afternoon teas.

Unfortunately, my relationship to cricket remained at best secondary and voyeuristic. I had of course played wind ball cricket like all other children, on the beach with the flattened lower end of the coconut branch cropped off for a bat and a tennis ball flying everywhere but forward and over in the breeze. In primary school, more sculpted wooden bats and less windy balls

Lovely Day – Gouache on paper – 4x5 ins – 2002

were used for serious matches between one school and the next and between different classes, but being the only child who wore thick-lens spectacles in the entire school, I was not the one selected or invited to play in the school-ground matches. They did agree though that I could keep the score, a concession I fully appreciated.

It was this limited 'bat and ball' exposure to the complex sport and my West Indianness that once nearly led me into a sticky wicket situation. While I was living in the Netherlands doing my Ph.D. in the late eighties, the event of the annual cricket game of staff against students arrived. The time had come for every ex-British colonial subject to stand up and be counted. A few of us around could actually lay claim to knowing the game. The boys approached me, cajoling, "But you come from the West Indies, from Trinidad, the land of C.L.R. James, the land of Gary Sobers and Viv Richards, you must be able to play cricket," they argued, mixing up geography and distance as if it were merely a boundary away. "Everyone from the West Indies plays cricket, don't they", the Indians from India argued. The South Africans were less convinced that this was so, but nonetheless joined in this plea to strengthen the puny student side at any cost. I was adamant. I stood my ground. "I will not only embarrass all of you, but more importantly myself and the various countries I represent" I retaliated, "but, I will be there in person and in spirit to support you nonetheless. I will make the tea for tea break and bring the obligatory cheese sandwiches." The game was played. The students lost miserably to a staff team that comprised a motley collection of ex-colonial ex-pats. Looking at them perform, I realised that I might have matched up to any member of the team who did represent us. The tea was soothing and sandwiches were gobbled up.

Ironically, it was an Englishman, my husband Rex, after all who made me really appreciate the finer points of the game of cricket – but I say 'appreciate' honestly as a voyeur of watching others for I cannot view an entire test match or series, at best a few exciting overs or two or four. I have learnt however to have an understanding and admiration of the skill and dexterity involved in bowling and batting, of the batsman nibbling the ball, and the tasks which a captain has of setting the field and determining order of batsmen or selecting the appropriate bowlers, to see the magic that can happen in a split second (in television replays of course), the subtle rules of the game, the power plays that mirror board room tactics, to delight in the comments from the cricket commentators, to recognise the individuality and personality of each team, each team member and each umpire for that matter, to understand the passion that it brings out in so many people over so many continents and to appreciate that this brief insight I have gained is but a blade of grass in the history of this complex field of sport.

Rex does not actually go to watch cricket at the Queen's Park Oval in Port of Spain or Sabina Park in Kingston or whatever grounds it is being played at. He prefers the comfort of his armchair in front of the television and the close up view of the field seen through the lens of the camera, the instant replays a few feet away from one's seat, or the radio commentary when there is no visual coverage. Queuing for bathrooms, drinks or food at the bar, lines of people waiting to get into or out of an oval, traffic jams to return home, is not part of the fun for him. Rather, he can plan his time at home carefully around the television coverage. His tea and lunch breaks coincide exactly with those of the players. When play is abandoned for poor weather he can get back to work, keeping an ear for the resumption of play or he continues reading his current book at hand. If a test match with England is on, he plans not just the day but also the week around cricket. It is a joy to watch him shadow playing each batsman, anticipating the bowler's curve, shouting with dismay at a dropped catch, a favourite riposte occasionally with passion "my mother could have hit that with a stick of rhubarb" when the batsman has missed a good ball. He has a stock of jokes that recur about commentators in the past, and can adopt many an English accent accurately, prodding Boycott with a "Yes, Geoffrey" in his best Yorkshire, or retelling a favourite quote from the drôle English commentator John Arlott, "There's a piece of paper blowing across the wicket and the umpire has walked over and picked up the paper and put it in his pocket". This commentator, a well-known wine connoisseur, would fill in gaps in the commentary with other equally inconsequential things that chanced around the cricket field during a match. A classic one, the day the batsman was the West Indian Michael Holding and the bowler, an Englishman surnamed Willey, Arlott was heard over the microphone, very loud and clear, observing "The batsman Holding the bowler's Willey" sending both the team of commentators and the crowd into spasms of laughter and offshoot puns for some time to come.

Watching Rex watch other teams at play I am struck by the concept of sportsmanship, the masculine respect for other men who excel at what they do. When the West Indies team is playing anyone else, he is their avid supporter. He has a fine appreciation of all teams and their best players.

However, he draws the line. When the English team plays, his mood is tactile, blithe happiness if they are winning, unmitigated depression if they are on a losing streak. This fierce nationalism is non-negotiable even after living more than two decades in the tropics. On the subject of cricket he and my father share a common language of communication, sometimes one of them voluntarily taking up the phone to playfully taunt the other when one or the other's team of choice is not doing so well. Let's face it; sports bring out the instincts of belonging and longing. How else could it have been manufactured into the passionate masculine battlefields and multimillion dollar industries both cricket and football have become.

Cricket remains in my view, despite the late twentieth century phase of the feminist revolution, a man's world. Women are primarily the voyeurs of the sport. This might explain why in one hundred years of cricketing stamps, there are only two with women on the image and one of these, a 40 cents St. Kitts stamps sports a jolly Queen Elizabeth the 2nd, presumably there not for her cricketing talent, the smile no doubt acknowledging a victory of the English cricketing team. Here I am very politically incorrect however, while grateful for the valuable protestations which women, many of them my colleagues, have made to be more visible in the game as players or actors of one sort or another, I prefer to remain the onlooker, looking on at the antics of the spectators seeing themselves on the big screen, deducing the unfolding narrative over time of how masculinity and nationalism is forever an ongoing game, played on many different fields and checking out the latest hairstyles and trouser fit of the cricketers.

There are many diversions after all within the sporting world.

August, 2008

Cricket Watching – Ink on paper – 9x6 ins – 2014

Trinidad

Exhibition blues

(for Nisha Hosein)
By Rex Dixon

The day of the exhibition dawned grey and wet
Rex got off the bed and started to fret
It will rain tonight and the crowd will be sparse
Don't make a long speech, he said, just finish up farse
They don't want to hear a treatise on painting
Next thing you'll have them tired and fainting
You academics love to hear yourselves talk
This time you just have to walk the walk
Don't go into technicalities or be profound
After all, they just want to hear another calypso sound.

October, 2008

Exhibition Blues – Acrylic on paper – 6x4 ins – 2010

The Netherlands

The Netherlands

Letter to Vincent
(For Els Mulder)

It is unfair to Vermeer and Rembrandt and the Van Dykes before them, and the host of great early and contemporary artists of The Netherlands, to single you out in this society, Vincent. The Netherlands for us has represented an open-ended banquet of visual possibilities from its musea and galleries to its rainbow fields of bloom. But you, Vincent, hold a special place in Rex's heart. Apart from a profound appreciation for your work, Rex has a dog-eared copy of your *Letters to Theo* from which he had memorized select passages such as, "*Dear Theo, I have lived on two slices of bread and half a glass of wine for the last three days, but I cannot go on without some lemon yellow, please send some more francs*". Whenever he needed to go shopping for more paint he often parodied this line into his own version but with the same pathos that connected you both across the years as struggling painters. As a young unemployed father in the sixties he had had to make decisions between buying the children a new pair of shoes and getting a tube of titanium white. He understood the lifeline that Theo had provided to you, and the loneliness and of the often-unrewarding profession you had both chosen. So Vincent, you became his reference point for The Netherlands even before he had made his first visit, next to our favourite Nederlander, the Curacao born Elizabeth Mulder Els had moved to The Netherlands in her late teens yet never forgot her Caribbean roots and any Caribbean islander who made it to Den Haag benefitted from her hospitality and kindness.

My own travels to your country Meneer Van Gogh began before Rex and I had met, in 1989 when I arrived in Den Haag at the Institute for Social Studies to do my doctoral studies. Els had become a close associate and friend by the time I returned with Rex first for my Ph.D. oral defence and

Cobra Group – Gouache on paper – 9x6 ins – 1995

Drawing for Hugo Claus – Gouache on paper – 11x11 ins – 1999

from 1995 onwards for a series of fellowships and study leaves. It was a pleasure to encounter your original work in person after countless years of starry starry night posters and poor reproductions of your sunflowers, to see the controlled savagery of your brushstrokes that put new tonalities of life into every blade of grass or object on your canvas.

The Via Galerie in Noordeinde, Den Haag, owned by Daniel Ridderplaat and his father Henk took a liking to Rex's paintings, which bore a strong resemblance to the Cobra school in which they specialized. So they took on Rex as one of their artists and by 1997 had given him his first show with this gallery. Rex could say that he owed many tubes of lemon yellow to you as one of his drawings, titled *Vincent in Den Haag*, was immediately snapped up by a gallery client. As an advertisement for another show, Daniel had hung one of Rex's large paintings on canvas in a glass case in the passageway to the Gallery. Someone seemed to have taken a liking to Rex's inimitable style or having read Daniel's deliberately slanted poster, associated Rex with the famous Cobra group Karel Appel, Corneille and Hugo Claus. So one Monday morning, after the show had been up for a week or two, the glass door was found swinging wide open and the painting was missing. To this day we have not found out who liberated the painting. Whoever it was had to use steel cutters to break the locks so it was a calculated theft and not a snatch and run affair. Somewhere in Den Haag or elsewhere today there is a Dixon masquerading as a Cobra masterpiece, vicarious fame after all. You would have appreciated this turn of events and the similarities here, selling only one painting during your lifetime Vincent, and given that your uniqueness was appreciated primarily by Theo while you were alive.

In 1999 I had travelled to Namibia alone to take a class of Namibian students to do research in Walvis Bay. That year we were doing research on sex workers. Rex made his way from Jamaica to Den Haag where we planned to meet up again. He was preparing for another Via Galerie exhibition so we decided he would go straight to Den Haag rather than come with me to Namibia this year. Els as usual came to the rescue finding him *gezellig* lodgings and looked after him until I arrived. Rex painted in the small hostel room, and was clearly missing me when he wrote me a postcard in doggerel in which you again figured in his subconscious.

"In Den Haag town I wander up and down
Wearing most days a smile, then a frown
Pondering about Vincent's ear
While waiting for the Indian girl to appear

I bought Van Gogh oil pastels which I use
And hardly ever go on the booze
And think of you in Walvis Bay
Watching the prostitutes night and day"

Els and her husband Harry van Starrenburg lived nearby the small seaside town of Scheveningen where you also once lodged and painted Sien Hoomik, the prostitute with whom you had formed a brief sympathetic alliance.

I had a small flat in Scheveningen during my first year in Den Haag and walking around this burg I learnt to recognize the faces from your paintings and those of Rembrandt and Vermeer in the Dutch men and women I would see each day. Harry was a retired merchant seaman with a passion for vintage radios and whisky, in this order. He had ended his sea faring days and spent much of his time poring over his radio collection, so we saw less of him, but Els was a partner on many of our forays in the Netherlands and joined us on several occasions in the Caribbean, including at our wedding in Jamaica.

Our companionship with Els went beyond the spiritual geography we shared. Like many Nederlanders we had met, she has a profound respect for painting and a strong sense of design and artistic balance. I remember on one of the first occasions when I was invited to Els's home for dinner, a newly arrived student then, I took her some light pink carnations, observing the beautiful tradition in this society of bringing flowers as a guest that I came to easily adopt. I would have chopped the ends of the long stems to equal length and dropped them in a tall vase, having not given much thought to the niceties of flower arrangement thus far. Els searched carefully in her cupboard and drew out a squat cylindrical cream porcelain vase and proceeded to artfully trim the stems at different lengths as she placed each flower carefully into the vase. The finished asymmetry of pink froth and pale green stems was exquisite against the fading light of a beautiful long summer evening and the bone white china of her tablecloth. Els's artistic sensibilities and understanding of beauty were as ingrained as were her unfaltering loyalty, friendship and constant kindness. If you found your support and solace in Theo, then as two *buitenlanders* in Holland dear Vincent, in Els, Rex and I had found our Theo.

June, 2001

Drawing for Vincent No 2 – Ink on paper – 6x4 ins – 1995

The Netherlands

Poem with no name

Van Bylandtstraat washed over in Payne's grey
A gloomy winter Sunday
On either side
aged houses sit like old men and women
rubbing shoulders and feet together
sending smoke signals through their chimney pipes
as if to say
there's life inside us still

Yesterday the shadows danced
mischievous dwarfs along your rooftops
Today the dull red bricks lie sullen
drugged dreamless,
too weary resisting
the damp and cold.

January, 2001

DEN HAAG
19. 7. 95

Drawing for Vincent No 1 – Ink on paper – 6x4 ins – 1995

England

England

Requiem for my grandfather

By Rex Dixon

Though the war had ended in 1945, London was in ruins well into the next decade. I was born in this city in 1939 at the outbreak of the Second World War and was evacuated to my paternal grandmother's place in rural Hertfordshire, thirty miles north of London. My mother and I had moved to the garden city where the Quaker financier, Ebenezer Howard, first created factories and housing estates with access to the Commons allocated for everyone to use as green space. There were swimming pools and tennis courts and bowling greens. It was a utopian vision so that working people would not end up in Victorian hovels of dirt and grime next to industrial factories.

My grandfather had survived the First World War, fighting in the trenches in France. He returned from the war and settled back into his working class routine in London only to experience a second war as a civilian in his hometown. It was my father who had to take up arms in the second war, posted to Mountbatten's fourteenth army in Burma. My mother Edna, although trained for domestic service as a young girl, after we moved to the Garden city found work in several factories. She made parachutes at the Spirella factory, a workshop that used to make nylons before the war. My mother told me that some of the factory girls used to put little notes into the parachutes for the airmen. I am not sure any of the men actually saw these notes, or, if they used the parachutes, that they had time for light reading as they hurriedly exited a burning airplane.

Sheltered in Letchworth, I was an only child and spent a lot of time reading, getting caught up in the *Swallows and Amazons* by J. Arthur Ransome, the school exploits of Billy Bunter, and comics Beano and Dandy

My mother Edna and her parents – Mixed Media – 8x6 ins – 2007

featuring characters like Desperate Dan and Keyhole Kate. My mother had an hour for lunch from the factory and she peeled the potatoes before she cycled to work in the morning, instructing me to put them on to boil at ten past twelve so they could be ready by half past twelve when she dashed back in for her lunch. If I was reading I would forget to put the potatoes on and many's the time I heard her coming through the gate and had not lit the gas and got told off as she could not have her lunch before she had to get back to work.

During the war it was illegal to have spare rooms, and living in my grandmother's house with three bedrooms, we had to take in lodgers brought from outside of Letchworth to work in the factories. A series of lodgers stayed for various periods. One was a Pole who had escaped from occupied Europe. I remember well an Irishman who painted scenes of his village – he was homesick and this was his way of bringing home to him. It was a watercolour of a little bridge with thatched cottages round the village green, very idyllic, quite unlike the style of painting to which I would later be attracted.

One day when I was six, my mother took me to the railway station and, coming out of the steam was this tall man in an army uniform with a long kit bag slung over his shoulder. He came up to us and started kissing my mother. "This is your father, Matthew", she said. I realized then that I was also named after him.

I had known he was returning as the streets were hung with red, white and blue bunting, there were street parties everywhere and there were other men coming home as well in the neighbourhood. In some homes the men did not return. But my father had become a stranger. I was only six months when he went off to war. He did not stay long with us. He said he could not settle down in the countryside and was going to London to look for work. He never came back.

In 1950 after I finished my infant education from the local village school in St. Nicholas Norton, I went to the grammar school in Letchworth town as I had passed the eleven plus exams. Only two of us passed this exam from the school. I had been made Head boy of St Nicholas Norton. I don't know why they bestowed this honour on me. Apart from bringing the frozen milk in each day and putting it in front of the coke stove, in the only other function I can recall being asked to fulfill in this role my performance was wanting. I was asked to write a letter to thank the village doctor, Dr. Wilson who had given a donation to the school. When I was told to go to the back of the classroom and write the letter I got cramps in my stomach and they had to send me home. The cramps disappeared mysteriously as soon as I got home.

I was a choir boy at St Nicholas Norton Church of England from age eleven and when my voice turned from soprano to tenor I was even made head choir boy. Letchworth in 1950s was not exactly swinging London so with time on my hands I also became a bell ringer, learning campanology. St Nicholas Norton Church had eight bells and as a boy you started on the treble and before long I was ringing in peals lasting up to three hours long and requiring an awful lot of stamina and concentration. By the time eight of us, I was the youngest of the lot, were finished with such a round, my hands

My Father when Young – Mixed Media – 9x6 ins – 2007

would be raw and blistered, painful for days after. When King George VI died, each village and city rang the bells half muffled to mourn his passing. And when Queen Elizabeth was crowned in 1952 we rang the bells again, this time in exultant peals. This high point of my campanology career is inscribed to this day inside the bell ringing chamber of the St Nicholas church on a wooden plaque, Rex Matthew Dixon, Treble, Age 11.

I was one of a few children in that street to go to grammar school. My mother was out of pocket from the expenses from this change in my status. She had to buy uniforms for the school, sportswear for rugby and physical education class, for woodwork you had to have an apron, and a satchel to carry books and a pencil case, the whole works. The woodwork teacher who taught part-time said to tell my mother he could get an apron from the school for me, but being a proud single mother she would not let me accept his charity. Kitted out in my new uniform after I had just started, my mother who was very proud of my achievement took me up to London to see Grandfather. He who had survived the trenches of France in the first world war, and the air raids in London of the second, now lived in his house in Peckham which had been bombed. The council had tried to move everyone out but he had refused to leave. They wanted to move him out to the pre-fabs in the suburbs. He was living in the basement of the bombed out building.

So we came off the train at King's Cross and I insisted we go to one of those little cafes just outside of the train station where you sit on the circular stools that go round and round to have a sticky bun and a cup of tea. Then we took the bus to Peckham. My mother had managed to buy two apples to take to my grandfather. I don't know how she got these as fruit was still very scarce at this time. We get to Peckham and walk down the steps into the cellar of the bombed building and there was Grandfather standing on his one good leg and a crutch, next to a pile of rubble which led up to the hole where the window used to be, the only source of light in the room. We did not stay long. We exchanged a few pleasantries and then Grandfather insisted on hobbling with us to the bus stop, me in my crisp new grammar school uniform with its blue blazer and embroidered *labora lude strenve* badge over the top pocket. As we waited on the bus, people passing up and down the street, my grandfather leant against the bus stop for support and started to serenade us with *The Lambeth Walk* accompanying himself with a pretend violin, the crutch now transformed into his bow. I looked up and down the street frantically, hoping the bus would come by soon. People walked by, some glanced at us questioningly, some smiled, some smirked thinking he was drunk. I wanted the pavement to swallow me up. It was the last time I saw him.

In 1986, painting in Jamaica in a small airless studio, I finally paid homage to my grandfather's memory and exorcised the shame of a foolish young boy with the painting, *The Pretend Violinist*.

January, 2016

The Pretend Violinist – Acrylic on canvas – 47x30 ins – 1986

England

Going to the Zoo

(For Christopher and Damon Dixon)
By Rex Dixon

Malcolm, Pat, me and Gru,
Went to see the lions at the Zoo
We went by train and by bus
We never even made a fuss
when we had to change at Elephant and Castle
though the drunks did make us startle
with their shouting and swearing
and their cans of lager bearing
because we were going to the zoo.
We walked in two by two
and when closing time at nearly dusk
it was only Pat and me who caught the bus.

London, Summer 1999

Going to the Zoo – Ink on paper – 9x12 ins – 2012

England

Oxford Musings

Yellow
Ochre
Brick
Like elegant sheaves of wheat
Stacked against an autumn sky.

City of spires, of sires and squires,
 Of cocky young men, with their heads in the air,
And streets that sing arias of Inspector Morse in despair

Thai Orchid and Opium Den restaurants now dot the space
Between Hotel Randolph and Kings Arms, they have found a place.
Passageways and halls of red snooty stone, giving way
to Oxford Brookes and lowered tone.

The graciousness of learning, of time honoured spent
Remains sealed in walls and guarded testaments
Released to the observant, the converted, the aware.
This medieval city of grace should prevail everywhere.

October, 2014

Oxford View – Ink on paper – 9x12 ins – 2016

Dreaming Spires – Ink on paper – 5x8 ins– 2016

England

Notes from a desperate evening in Lumb Bank, Yorkshire

"You have Ted Hughes room" Jill says.
Perhaps she tells everyone this, inspirational kindness in a lie
Offering a cup of welcome tea
which I drink in a Wuthering Heights mug
to match the misty summer day in Bronteland

A black and white photo of Anthony Minghella
stares into my eyes, prompting words out of images.
Yet faded verses coffined behind glass render up ghosts,
Rather than prose
that sits too lumpy in my chest.

The evening light lowers itself on the horizon
Selfishly guarding favours of summer heat.
A variegated green carpet lies over distant hills
Patterned by drystone walls
That someone's great great grandfather built;
Perhaps Edmund Wadsworth, born 1846 of Richard and Louisa
who lies buried
in the Heptonstall graveyard.
Lives recorded on tablets of writing stone
that remind us to
forget the present.

Haworth Graveyard – Mixed Media – 8x12 ins – 2008

Here she sits
In the year of our lord
With the curve of a hand
Matching shape against shape
Mining darkness from light
For the pleasure of the word
in the shadow of others
before me
at Lumb Bank

June, 2015

Canada

Canada

A world on a little hill

Rex travelled with me to Canada where this was delivered as a dinner speech at a fundraising event of the Toronto Naparima Girls' Alumni.

It's five minutes to eight. A sunny Monday morning in San Fernando, Trinidad. Krishna, the driver of the sluggish capacious black Vauxhall, drops me in front of the Susamachar church, on Carib Street. This is convenient for him – he had rounds to make still to St. Joseph's Girls Convent on the Harris Promenade and to Naparima Boys College in Paradise Pasture, a further half mile away, to drop off the others he chauffeured from the quaint little suburb of Princes Town each school day. But this was not at all convenient for me!

To arrive in time for morning assembly at Naparima Girls' High School, summoned by the first bell at eight a.m. sharp, I had to walk from Carib Street, across Coffee Street (images of beer and coffee as distant then as it is redolent now) to the bottom of La Pique Road, and climb the steep hill to reach the school yard. The school buildings burrowed snugly into the side of the hill, as if some female animal had made a safe and warm nest for her young. If by chance I managed to get there before the bell, I would still need to unceremoniously fling my bag down, grab bible and hymn book from my desk and join the punctual ones. On the sound of the whistle, chattering scores of girls under the spreading tamarind tree would order themselves by class and march in army lines of two to Beethoven's *Fur Elise* or *Onward Christian Soldiers*, depending on the mood of the pianist that day, into the auditorium for morning assembly and worship.

Many a morning, needless to say, I did not make that procession. Half way up the hill, pearls of sweat already beading my upper lip and neck, the too heavy book bag and the weighty navy blue pleated serge skirt, regulation two inches under the knee, presented a major handicap in this race against time. I would make an informed; some might say pragmatic, decision and head for the 'late room', conveniently located on the ground floor of the most easterly wing of the school. It was a dark cheerless room, full of silent guilt and repentant female souls, monitored by a different schoolmistress on duty each week. This hour away from Presbyterian assembly where the rest of the early birds were communing with their maker, was, however, the perfect time to catch up with unfinished homework or, better yet, to plunge back into the compelling novel or steamy romance. I can admit only now, long past the lingering fear of penalties, that any novel I was then reading was papered over with brown paper labeled *My First Latin Reader* in bold ink, in case of prying eyes. I have often wondered how neither my parents nor my teachers ever cottoned on to my preoccupation with reading Latin. But I did win the school prize for Latin in my O'Level year – as if by some process of osmosis this bounteous dead language had seeped into my consciousness. If it were not for the black marks against my name and school house for late coming, spending an hour in the late room was not at all an unpleasant way to begin the day. In fact, I would recommend it highly to others if the practice of the 'late room' still obtains – I think it was crucial to the fine tuning of a mind that very early had grasped the pleasure and danger of resisting authority and convention.

While I didn't support Krishna's nonchalant attitude to my terror of the school bell, there were other benefits to late coming. At about three minutes to eight, when I was dashing around the Esso station about midway to my finish line, a young school boy would bend the corner of High Street, heading for Presentation College – the Catholic boys school that literally rubbed shoulders with Naps Girls. The young man was also wending his late way to school. I admired his careless gait in the face of ticking second hands, his finely chiseled features and curly hair and, possibly, the seams of his well fitted grey trousers. This made my day. I gathered that he played on the Presentation College football team but I never ventured near a match, preserving for the benefit of my friends a pro-bookish stance that was my trademark – in reality my father would not have allowed me to go un-chaperoned to an inter-college football match anyway. Nonetheless, investing him with qualities I am pretty sure he could not have possessed, the

Driving Miss Patsy – Mixed Media – 10x7 ins – 2016

male heroes in the novels I was reading moved from the realm of the abstract and took on more concrete features. I found out his name from the Presentation College magazine but I never made any attempt to speak to him. Well brought up girls, particularly of the Naps Girls variety, were to be circumspect, dignified and always beyond reproach, keep it cool, keep it covered and keep it clean.

I started high school in 1964, the final year in which Ms. Margaret Scrimgeour held the post of Principal. She was the last of the expatriate Canadian female principals. Physically, she presented the archetypal missionary woman, tall and angular, pale white skin, by then a bun tightly pulling back her silvering hair. In this year of leadership she was still full of energy and drive, an ageless woman. Ms. Beulah Meghu, our first female principal of Indian origin, succeeded her. Only in retrospect did I understand what an interesting period we experienced at Naparima Girls' in these transitional years, or for that matter how knowledge was being conveyed in the most non-traditional ways, providing valuable lessons that have resonated in my life and work since, in unquantifiable ways.

The school was then, perhaps still, Indian female dominated – after all it was set up by the Canadian Presbyterian missionaries in the first decade of the twentieth century to encourage Indian parents to send their girls for further education where they would be protected from the too open gaze of a multicultural society. The long wooden colonial style dormitory building was an ever-present visual reminder of the days when girls who lived far away were housed on site. As were the two still resident Canadian teachers Constance Wagar and Joy Vickery who lived in an apartment at the end of the dormitory building. Tossing this memory around now, I realized that the idea of the expatriate missionaries as caretakers and colonial mistresses of our education blended imperceptibly and perhaps without conflict or confrontation with the homegrown and homespun familiarity of Trinidadian female teachers. The existence of chapters of Naps Girls' alumni in Canada is a poignant yet defiant testimony to a Canadian missionary experiment begun in the small outpost of Trinidad in 1868.

The school's curriculum was a marriage of different worlds – the domestic and public, the foreign and local, the Christian and non-Christian, the formal academic with the extra-curricular.

One interesting example comes from the emphasis on the domestic arts, needlework and cookery (definitely then not given the misnomer of domestic science). It's become fashionable for women to say things like, "I can't cook to save my life", or "I don't know how to boil water" and let's face it, most of us don't really ever have to sew a button on again. Perhaps an understandable sentiment in this day and age when women have rebelled against the tyranny of the kitchen stove or the drudgery of the assembly line. But I honestly enjoyed these subjects and have wonderful memories of the tutorship of the women who led us gently through this phase where we were being groomed for occupations beyond that of "being barefoot and pregnant".

I forgot who taught us sewing in the first form, I think it was a Ms. Greaves. One day the homework assignment was to do a buttonhole by hand. I took it home and my mother, who was superb at needlework, took the white piece of folded cotton and stitched a perfectly symmetrical magenta pink buttonhole of about half inch in length. I brought it back to school the next day and handed it up very confidently in my specimen book. Shortly after examining the books, the teacher called me up to the front desk.

"You didn't do this homework on your own did you?" she asked.
"No, miss, my mother helped me," I said, very proudly. I don't think at this age of barely eleven it entered my head that there was an ethical issue here – as far as I understood it, my mother like any good parent was simply making sure she was helping me do my homework.

"It is very lovely," Miss said gently, with a wry smile playing around her lips. "Your mother is a good seamstress, but you have to do it by yourself this time".

I have never forgotten that lesson, the kindness with which Ms. Greaves conveyed in an understated way that while my overprotective mother had pastoral care over me as a child, I now needed to do things on my own and to learn how to make my own way in the world. My buttonhole was a seriously more jiggled one, not completely clean around the edges, a postmodern abstraction compared to my mother's neatly ordered stitches.   I still have in my possession this notebook with both specimens attached which my mother also dutifully kept for me all these decades long.

Like sewing, cookery classes at Naparima Girls' were a pleasure rather than penance, as it's popularly perceived now. While instructing us in methods of preparing food, Mrs. Bissessar taught a lot of other wholesome values. She transmitted the artistry of cooking rather than its functionality. Little pats of butter were dotted evenly into the creamy dough in the making of oh so flaky pastry, the slab of beef was gently rubbed with a dampened towel and cubed into even pieces, glowing healthily red in the bowl while waiting to be seasoned with fresh green basil, thyme and cloves of redolent garlic before being tender stewed creole style. The local fruits like mangoes, pommeracs and mammy apple were diced evenly and matched for colour and texture before they were mixed with syrup and just the barest hint of Trinidad rum to produce the desserts. Nationalism and economy were taught in the kitchen as much as in the classroom. If you were lucky enough to be selected on the roster to shop for the ingredients for that day's lesson, you would be sent with carrier bag and some funds to the market on Mucurapo Street (and legitimately miss that morning's worship assembly). Kamala Vasanti (Vas) Boochoon, a lifelong friend who started Naps Girls the same day I did and left the same time, agreed that cookery classes and thrifty market expeditions were prominent and enjoyable in her memory. We learnt to look dead fish in the eyes, to be firm yet gentle when pressing flesh, to examine the texture and colour of the vegetables to judge their crispness, to buy what was in season and freshly grown by our gardeners, lessons which have served me, needless to say outside of the kitchen as well. There is more to cookery than meets the eye.

Rhoda Reddock, a colleague of mine who is a Bishop Anstey girl, has commented on many an occasion that she has not met a Naps girl, well certainly none of our generation, who was not a good cook. It was no surprise that the Naparima Girls' High School Cookbook produced by some devoted ex-teachers and students became a best seller, funding another wing or two to the school buildings and selling as a preferred local cookbook and a gift to visitors and Trinis abroad. It truly represents a home-baked slice of Trinidad culture and the country's cuisine at its best.

While formal lessons and examinations have all slipped into an amnesiac whole, the bell of memory clangs more vibrantly around incidents or events that broke the routine of the everyday. One year around Carnival someone had invited the calypsonian Slinger Francisco – The Mighty Sparrow – to the school as a special treat and he was so thoroughly charming and wickedly entertaining, we were hooked for life by this art form. A red letter day was the visit of the then budding poet Derek Walcott to a literature class in the sixth form, invited to speak to us informally about writing and poetry. Through art classes we visited the sculpture studios of Ralph and Vera Baney and through the annual presentation of dramatic plays, the classics like Longfellow's *Hiawatha* and Oscar Wilde's *The Importance of Being Earnest*, moved from the printed page into our everyday vocabulary, shaping literary and artistic sensibilities that were vital to the expanding mind.

One red letter day, Ms. Meghu our Principal and then General Paper teacher of the sixth form was followed into the classroom by the office attendant who was armed with two large cardboard boxes full of books. Ms. Meghu had combed her own library and selected a wide range of authors to whom she thought we should be exposed. By this time, I had exhausted all the fiction at the school library, had selectively read all the romances on the shelves of the Harris Promenade Carnegie library, had been systematically working through authors in alphabetical order at the public library in Princes Town and was fast progressing through the Ws. It was a major revelation and relief that there were other authors whom we had not encountered, not yet on local reading lists, like V. S. Naipaul and Samuel Selvon. As good teachers always are, Ms. Meghu was prescient about our futures, understanding that already from our classrooms would come the new generation of writers like Shani Mootoo, Dionne Brand, Ramabai Espinet – all past students of Naparima Girls' and all of whom, incidentally, have migrated to Canada.

Naparima Girls' chauffeured many born in my age and time from adolescence into young womanhood, in an extraordinary fashion. We learnt the art of becoming women, comprehending as one invariably does in an all girl's school the wiles known to womanhood, but never focused on these arts as a means to an end. The no-nonsense attitude of our teachers, the competitiveness for excellence fostered among students, the challenges for us to be creative and original, seeped into our bloodstream, in an atmosphere that was natural, surrounded as we were with nature in its finest forms, a circular plateau on the hillside, squirrels scampering up the slope, lush tropical trees and vines vying to enter the classrooms closest to the forest. We were set above the little town of San Fernando, of it but apart, reaching for stardom while perched on a plateau on this hill.

I still cannot arrive in good time for anything that is ordered or rigid – preferring the meandering pathway of individuality and thought to the straight line of conformity. But somehow, between the insistent bells and the exploratory classroom, I was given the best of both worlds – discipline yet unconstrained freedom, in this remarkable place I was privileged to occupy for a brief but adventurous time on this world on a little hill.

June, 2011

Toronto Tower Block – Mixed Media – 12x8 ins – 2011

SAFARI HOTEL WINDHOEK NAMIBIA

Scenes of NAMIBIA: Termite Hill. 25.6.98.
They are very common in the northern half of the country.
This hill is 4 meters high. They can be taller.
In der nördlichen Hälfte des Landes sind die Termitenhügel
häufig. Dieser ist 4 m hoch. Sie können viel größer sein.

Photo: H.W. Thomas

Namibia

Namibia

Reluctant Tourists

Rex writing notes to himself while drinking beer after beer in an Ondangwa bottle shop.

"Plastic bags and gravestones bare
You're not supposed to point your finger there
Plenty desert sand, no desert rose
All that sand gets up your nose"

He was waiting for me to have my hair braided. This is no mean task to accomplish. The two nice young ladies took over five hours to carefully cane row and wrap extensions with black thread to contain the straight ends sticking out everywhere. The cemetery was across the road from the bottle shop and the hairdresser. Rex said he watched over ten funerals in this time and was told by the shop owner as he was inquiring why they had so many funerals in one morning not to point his finger at the cemetery as it would bring him bad luck.

But so far, this was Rex's second visit and my third summer in Namibia, and we had had only good fortune, watched over by Meme Eunice and Anna, her driver. I had been invited to teach for three summers from 1998 to 2000 at the University of Namibia through a gender studies project of the Netherlands Institute of Social Studies, my doctoral *alma mater*. Eunice had done her masters at this Institute many years ago and now headed the project to introduce women and gender studies to Namibia. Rex accompanied me on two of the three trips, and never let me forget that he missed out on the best one, the time we took the gender research methodology class to

Patsy's Braiding – Mixed Media – 9x8 ins – 2000

Walvis Bay to do participant observation on prostitution in the coastal town. The fieldwork was done in bars and nightclubs, so you could forgive him this grudge.

He liked the trip up north however, to Ondangwa and Oshakati, towns near the Angolan border. We crossed over to Angola one day. It was exactly the same on the other side of the rough border fence. We had taken the students to carry out ethnographic research on the kraals in the suburbs of

The Reluctant Tourist – Acrylic on canvas – 65x40 ins – 1999

The Women listen to the Mayor – Mixed Media – 12x8 ins– 2000

Oshilumbu Visit the Headman – Mixed Media – 12x8 ins – 2000

the townships of Oshakati and Ondangwa. In the course of our research we had to negotiate good will through the chief who possessed two wives and were honoured with an invitation to their home, a series of connected kraals each of which housed another domestic function of the extended household. Dinner was an interesting affair. There was chicken stew very tasty and spicy set in a carved wooden bowl, served with steamed *mahangu* (pearl millet) and cold homemade beer. Now the manner of keeping the beer cold was what fascinated Rex. The floor of the kraal was made of sand, not unlike sea sand, the dominant soil type of most of Namibia. The wives had dug a hole about two feet wide and one foot deep in the middle of the kraal floor and they placed a round earthenware container full of beer into the hole and patted about six inches of a mixture of wet sand around the sides of the earthenware container. The top was left open and wooden beer mugs were used to dip out draughts for the drinker. The beer was cool but sandy. Despite the gritty texture, Rex enjoyed the chance to sample another homemade brew.

I imagine all chauffeurs have a strong constitution and powers of concentration. Anna was a champ. On the third summer to Namibia, the morning after we had arrived, as usual via Capetown then Windhoek the night before, Anna picked us up at the Safari Hotel, a place we began to call home on our trips to Namibia, and together with Meme Eunice we started a 750 kilometre trek up to Ondangwa. We stopped in one town only for food and drink but along the way Anna and Meme Eunice kept their energies going with biltong, one of the many varieties. They were sampling today preserved ostrich and beef. We tried some but did not get the hang of it although both women managed to chew their way for hundreds of kilometres. We had to get to the Cresta Lodge Hotel by sundown, so Anna allowed me one more stop when I had my first sight of giraffes in the wild, picking at the leaves on the tree tops as if they were grazing grass on a field, gawky, graceful creatures with soft innocent looking eyes. For some reason their eyes also reminded me of Anna's dark brown ones that you knew you could trust. But we had also one day seen Anna demolish some men in a bottle shop with fast words and those eyes turned into flashing steel black.

Eunice was the force to be reckoned with. She was passionately nationalistic in post-independence Namibia. Although we grasped, in the relatively brief time that we spent there, some of the politics of nationhood, as with all visitors we barely scratched the surface of this understanding. Originally called South-West Africa, Namibia was a German colony from

The wind blows the sand in spirals and gusts on both sides of the border

R.D. 00

Border Crossing - Gouache on paper – 4x6 ins – 2000

1884, with South African mandated by the League of Nations to administer the territory following world war two, and, after joint South African and competing German interests from 1946 onwards, became independent in March 1990, only nine years before our first visit. At independence the name Namibia was chosen because of the Namib Desert that ran along the western Atlantic length of the country. This desert had 'saved' this country from its earliest encroachment when the Portuguese landed in the fifteenth century, one of their earliest explorations; at a site they named Cabo da Cruz, or Cape Cross. The explorers were not equipped to face the scale of sand and emptiness, land which provided you with no markers of location or natural vegetation on which to survive. Today, after over a century of German rule, relations between the ethnic groups that comprise the country, among them the Herero, Himba, Ovambo. Damara, Nama, Kavango, the San (Bushmen), the Rehoboth Basters, the Coloureds, the Whites, the Caprivian, Topnaars, and the Tswana are peaceful. The ousted commercial and industrial owners felt dis-empowered and resentful while they continued their ventures. Communication still took place in thirty different languages the most dominant among them and language of officialdom and commerce were Deutsch, Afrikaans and English or a combination of these referred to as Namlish. Eunice could wrap her tongue around many of the languages but she was fierce about what could be spoken or not when she confronted those of German origin. She took us to the Cape Cross seal reserve, still home to one of the largest colony of brown seals. The cross signifying the Portuguese landing was still standing as a mark of their first attempt at possession. In 1999, apart from thousands of languishing seals, mothering their seal babies in and out of the water, noisy and not a little smelly, the entrance booth and little gift shop were manned by a white couple. As we entered and attempted to pay for our viewing privileges, they looked at Rex and assuming common ethnic roots, immediately spoke to him in Afrikaans. Meme Eunice put a stop to the transaction at once. She confronted the couple head on. "Did you not know that the language of this country is now English?" she said. "We do not speak Afrikaans here again. And these are my visitors, they are English speaking. You will speak to them in English". And so we bought our tickets from two mute ticket sellers.

She and Anna bundled us off to Swakopmund as a break from the teaching and as part of the natural hospitality. Swakopmund was Namibia's premier holiday resort on the Atlantic coast, not unlike the seaside resort of Brighton except with bigger waves, sandy roads, colonial hotels and a large very warm orange sun at setting time. Anna usually disappeared as soon as she deposited us. The next day was carnival in Swakopmund. The early morning parade of open back trucks with masked white folk reminded me of what I had read about early carnival in Port of Spain where the middle and upper classes were on floats while the common man and woman cavorted in the streets. What was different about this one was that young black Namibian boys were picking up coins and sweets tossed to them by the whites and coloureds on the back of the trucks. Eunice did not take kindly to this. Hands on her broad hips, voice raised to a higher than normal pitch, she berated the little boys for the handouts, admonishing them to throw it back.

"Do not take the money or the sweets" she adjured loudly, to no one in particular, as the boys were really not taking her on.

"Throw it back to them, throw it back," she shouted over the din of music and revelry, as she made puny attempts to practice what she preached.

Eunice took us to see the dunes of the Namib Desert. I had never before envisioned the unique beauty of a desert. The word desert conjures

Dune No 7 – Acrylic on paper – 14x10 ins – 2011

barrenness and desolation. Instead, we confronted the vastness of a landscape, wide open to the bright blue sky, the spongy smoothness of the sand hills, concave shapes that seemed to sway with the wind, changing form and colour as the contours catch light, from lemon yellow to cadmium to ochre and sienna. Notwithstanding its mesmerizing grandeur, as you drive past dune to dune, the expanse is repetitive. Yet Anna kept driving and driving as if there were some purpose to this desert outing. I half expected as one does in the old movies to come across an oasis with short palm trees and a liquid pond and camels lounging around the edges of the water. But Eunice clearly had a plan. As we approached yet another dune, she cried out to Anna, "Stop, stop here". She got out of the four-wheel drive and looked and looked at the magnificent dune in front of us, the sides of which some people were trying to scale.

"Ach," she said regretfully. "Dune Number 7 has got smaller".

We had never thought that the shifting sands would change the feel of the landscape, nor that the dunes, like mountains, were actually recognizable and named. More appealing to see in Eunice was the expression of fondness for an inanimate object and for a landscape that seemed unmarked to the outsider but to the insider offered infinite differences, a nation's geography they could hold with affection.

Rex discovered the work of John Muafangejo in the National Museum in Windhoek. Muafangejo died fairly young at age 44, in 1987, and produced work that has been collected since 1968. The first Namibian artist to be formally recognized as a gallery artist, he was the first to bring Namibian concerns of culture and politics into the format of gallery art through his training in printmaking, painting and weaving, which he somehow combined in the form of linocuts. Rex liked his mixture of text and image, their humour and pathos and the unusual compositions. Not unlike Haitian and Australian aboriginal art there is similarity in the alternating usage of negative and positive space against the picture plane. His restriction of his prints to only black and white makes the work more powerful and dramatic. Muafangejo's catalogue remains a well-thumbed one on our bookshelf.

Anna drove us back to Windhoek that summer, she and Eunice chewing away at biltong and drinking beer. Altogether we had spent a lot of time with Anna who took us to the grocery, or to shops when we needed to, would accompany the students on field trips and once on the way back from class took us to visit her family in Katutura, amidst this teeming township of cheek

Art Gallery at Windhoek – Mixed Media – 12x16 ins – 1999

by jowl housing and overactive street life. A few years later we heard from Immaculate, a well-proportioned Namibian woman who had also been a student of the programme at the Institute of Social Studies. Immaculate worked as one of the tutors of the course that I taught each year in Namibia. She wrote to tell us that Anna had died.

January, 2016

Seville

Seville

Viva Seville,
Viva Ogden Nash

Seville is the place to bare
The midriff, arm and brassiere
The sun is hot , the days are long
I don't fit in, my shape is wrong

Tristeza is not la palabra for this city
Pero las otras muchachas, they look far too pretty
I decide no está bien to feed on despair
Perhaps its time I let down my hair

The bodegas spill over on the sidewalks after siesta
They turn each day into a Spanish fiesta
We wonder why there are few street cafes in Port of Spain
It must be the traffic, surely not fear of rain

The tourists they come from near and far
To sample every tapas bar
Olives, gamba, pescado frito
Calamari, cerdo, salchicha y queso

The Spanish waiters dress in white and black
They're swift on their feet, there's never a slack
The cervezas y vino, sirven como si en dolor
Tal vez demasiado turistas, o tal vez el calor

Spanish Postcard – Pencil on paper – 4x6 ins – 2000

Vasos de sangria go down one by one
Pretty soon, you look up, and so has the sun
You stand on your feet and they begin to wobble
It's then you find out, you're really in trouble

Es hora de sentarse and order otro plato de tapas
'Cos tomorrow en los Archivos, you can't read the mapas
The world stops spinning, you begin to slow down
You decide after all that you quite like this town.

September, 2000

Seville

Hotel Inglaterra
(By Rex Dixon)

Seville is a town
Which gets up late
The sun in the day
would make you faint
Through the narrow streets
we wander
      up and down
looking in vain for a
      MOORISH

FROWN.
HOTEL INGLATERRA
SEVILLE.
2000
Rex Dixon.

Hotel Inglaterra View No 1 – Pencil on paper – 4x6 ins – 2000

Hotel Inglaterra View No 2 – Pencil on paper – 4x6 ins – 2000

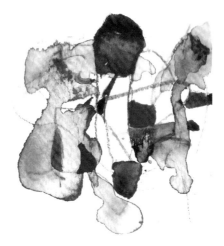

Japan

Japan

Domo arigato –
Japanese kanji

Domo arigato
Japanese kanji
Engraved in memory

Tea gardens
Moss green stony trails of flowing water
Invisible orchestration of nature
In an unbroken chain

R.D.00

Shinto worship
Draw water from a stone basin
Purify hands
Ring in the gods

Train ride from Osaka
White gloves appear through sliding doors
A conductor bows
Second nature

Kimono girl in Kyoto station
Delicately arranged orange blossom white
On a crowded escalator
Composure ascending

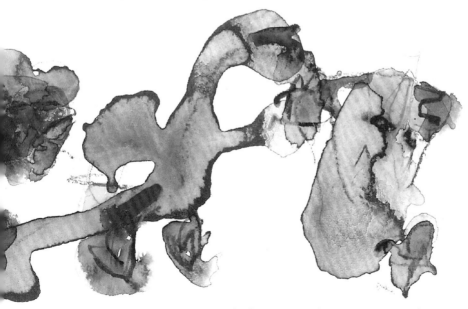

Japanese Sketch No 1 – Gouache on paper – 4x12 inches – 2000

Amusement arcade
Two toned young boys with coloured hair
Gangling arms and legs
Machined to obey

Rice wine, Sushi and you
Slabs of fish on sticky rice
Hands warming around a porcelain jug
Happiness glows

Modernity in stripes
Observe the light
Keep to the right
Zebra crossing

Kyoto Memory – Ink on paper – 8x6 ins – 2016

Haiti

Haiti

Hayti, I'm Sorry

This was written in 2001 before the earthquake in 2010 that reduced Port au Prince to rubble. I returned to Haiti in June 2016 and feel that much of this analysis still applies.

Haiti is not a place for the squeamish or the unseasoned traveler. "*Attendez derriere la ligne jaune* – Wait behind the yellow line" the sign says when you manage to find your way through the chaotic two and three headed snaky lines and get up to the glass fronted airport cubicles of the Haitian immigration officers. Surprisingly, the immigration officials waited patiently for the incoming visitor or returning Haitian. But no one stayed behind the line. The line was not even yellow. It was more of jaundiced ochre, trampled over by hundreds of feet of laden travelers. Waiting for the luggage is yet another Haitian experience – the conveyor belt resembles a chaotic Dambala (African snake god) going round and round, a humped back snake misshapen by cello taped and stringed up broken cardboard boxes, oversized and travel weary suitcases, even large bottles of potable water clothed in soiled linen. "Sorry to greet you in this condition", a sign apologizes above the hot, crowded steamy baggage area with one ineffectual fan swirling the heat around unevenly, "we are in the process of rectifying it". Signs of rectification were hard to identify in the arrival lounge in 2001.

Armed with one state of the art laptop computer, three cameras and two smallish suitcases, our response of "vacance" to the customs' officer conventional question "What eez the purpose of your vizeet to 'Ayti" was understandably greeted skeptically. He looked over our heads to the search officer, "Pleez opaan ze baggaages". He rustled through the spare packaging of

116

Three Loas Tap-Tap – Mixed Media – 11x8 ins – 2005

clothes and essentials and helped politely to close the suitcase as he waved us royally on. His courtesy reminded me of my sister's comment from her visit to Haiti a few years before. Despite their depressed living conditions, she had found Haitians to be a polite and extremely kind people. So far so good.

You manage to find a path through customs into another set of indeterminate lines, pass the exit door held open by a large rock stone on one side. A yellow hot midday sun against a sea of black faces, most of them self employed porters vying and trying for your attention, struggling to get a hand on your baggage. Others shouting *taxee taxee*, others waiting for relatives or friends and obscuring an escape route. Yet there was some method in this madness, the Montana had come to Mohammed. The hotel driver had turned up to meet us.

I had come to Haiti, accompanied by Rex, to carry out research for my book on Caribbean iconography. Minus one or two islands here and there, over the last two decades I had traveled throughout most of the Caribbean, including to the Dominican Republic, which adjoins Haiti. Haiti was still unknown territory within the Region. Columbus had claimed the entire island for the Spanish crown back in 1492, calling it Hispaniola or little Spain. The island was later called Santo Domingo by the Spanish, who began introducing African slaves into the colony from 1503. By 1635 the French had settled the western side and of course translated the name into their tongue, Ste Domingue. A campaign of terror through poisoning against white colonials led by maroon Francois Makandal began in 1750 in the Bois Caiman. The real war however, was fought consistently from 1791 to 1803, with indescribable bloodshed and intrigue, plots and counterplots, between white colonials and white planters, between small planters and big planters, between white planters and mulattos, and against the mulatto and black population. The events in Ste Domingue were spurred on by the revolution in France in 1789 for *liberté, egalité* and *fraternité*. The French and the British became strange bedfellows in the attempt to suppress the uprisings in Ste Domingue. Despite the odds the black slaves and some of their half brothers, the mulattos, had fought and won the first successful slave revolution. In 1803, in a gesture of defiance and vision, Jean-Jacques Dessalines, one of the black generals, ripped out the white from the French flag, symbolically tearing out the white control, and with independence in 1804 returned the name given to the land by the Tainos, "Hayti – the land of mountains", to itself. In 1804, while the slave trade and slave labour persisted in other colonies, the Haitian population had thrown off this shackle, as David Rudder, Trinidadian calypsonian sang, "back in those days when black men knew their place was in the back". As voiced by Rudder, however, a nagging thought persists. Is Haiti still paying the price for this audacity?

Montana Dream – Ink on paper – 12x10 ins – 2004

It is impossible to imagine the Haiti of today outside of Haiti, despite the anecdotes of visitors, the discussions with Haitians, the documentaries and news coverage or books one has read. These convey a narrative of endless pillaging by a string of dictators from the nineteenth century onwards, widespread violence and political intrigue, a legendary poverty of boat peoples who have risked their lives to find refuge in the United States, Jamaica and Cuba. Such stories go hand in hand with another face of Haiti, about the superb French cuisine in the restaurants of Petionville, an abundance of naïve artists and creativity, a society of rich tradition, steeped in vodou and blended Catholicism. A nation of extremes, extreme grandeur of ideas and struggle, extreme wealth and extreme poverty.

Of these, the poverty of the darkest people of Haiti is the most self-evident. The light yellow population is barely visible sheltered behind stone walls and well guarded fences. There is no dignity in poverty. It cows the human spirit and defiles space. The majority of people are forced to live hand to mouth from day to day in overcrowded uninhabitable shacks or unfinished concrete structures. Over two million people live in Port au Prince, in a geographic space barely more than the city and suburbs of Port of Spain. Many of the roads are gravel tracks; the atmosphere is thick with yellow dust and despair. I could not add insult to injury and assume the stance of the modern day missionary, sociologist or anthropologist focusing a prurient lens on the poverty or quaint customs of Haitian peoples nor the indignation of a glorified sanitary inspector. Like all societies Haiti is riddled with contradiction and complications, which the short-term visitor can never comprehend. I could not take photographs of the swarming streets and the festering rubbish piles. Nonetheless, the scenes not photographed linger, inscribed in the retina of memory. A young boy, not more than seven or perhaps eight, stooped over a side walk drain in down town Port au Prince, clearing away the debris as if removing topsoil, and with a dirty plastic cup filling an equally dirty plastic bucket. I asked what he was doing. "To wash ze cars weeth" was the reply. For the cars themselves constantly dust covered from the unpaved streets, it seemed an appropriate enough solution. Another scene in Cap Haitien to the north, where the fiercest battles were fought in this place once called Cap Francois and considered the Paris of the Caribbean. We come out of the small airplane onto the tarmac and before we can make it the few yards to the modest wooden building, about ten poorly clothed men, fighting and clawing at each other like tom cats, quarrel to grab

To Cap-Haitien – Ink on paper – 12x10 ins– 2004

our baggage tags so that they can be paid a tip to retrieve our luggage. We drive past the coal market in the center of town. Young and old, indiscernible from the bags of coal dust and the dusky grey-black, which settles over every object and every moving creature, as if already burying Haiti alive. Dante's inferno comes to mind.

The Lonely Planet series, a sensitive guidebook, had suggested that it was not kind to photograph the misery and poverty of the Haitian peoples. It is *d'accord* to capture the resilience and creativity of the Haitians, but not their shame. Jean Claude our guide and chauffeur advised that it would be wiser to take photographs discreetly if we wanted to, but he was clearly not in favour as well. I agreed. For me, photographs seemed treacherous to the courage and vision of the events two centuries ago, disloyal to those Haitians who are still fighting bravely in so many different ways. Perhaps my attitude is self-righteous, a self-righteousness of yet another kind. But Haiti does not need the indignation of one more peripatetic visitor. It needs schools, and health centers, running water and roads, and jobs to go around for the millions of people who live cheek by jowl, from hand to mouth each day. It needs and partially survives on the services of some well-disposed aid officials and entrepreneurs who stay in the healthy mountain slope hotels (as I did), while they dispense relief of all kinds. One young woman we met in the hotel had come to Haiti for three months under the Pan American Health Organization to monitor the polio vaccine immunization programme among the young children. Another young American girl age 22, not too long graduated from Emory University, and had come to work in the orphanages in the north. She said it was heart-rending work; you dealt with forty cases of under-nourished diseased infants in the clinics, and walk outside and there were forty-five more.

Then there is the other side of Haiti, which has weaved its myth and cast its voodoo spell, a narrative of creativity out of despair, the lotus blooming on the dunghill. This, too, is also one-track, too gratuitous. The sidewalks of far too many simplistic and repetitive canvasses, the painted tap-taps, beautifully designed but always over stuffed with passengers, the derivative ironwork of exploited vodou themes. Poverty and an indiscriminate market have done little for art other than creating another artifice. Too Naipaulian a vision perhaps? Yes and no. Yes, there has emerged a wonderful sense of the untutored line and a primary use of colour among the naïve artist and voodoo art objects, as if the denuded mountain tops, flora and fauna and

Baron Samedi – Ink on paper – 12x10 ins– 2014

peoples stripped of decent livelihoods must declare themselves through an imaginary Joseph's coat. There has admittedly emerged something which is popularly called Haitian art, a recognizable aesthetic of shape, color and form referred to as Haitian, largely due again to the "discovery" of "primitive" Haitian painters like Hector Hypolyte and Philome Obin by American and French intellectuals and artists in the 1940s. In an art world always seeking fresh blood, Haitian art has emerged in the twentieth century as new and original. On the heels of early twentieth century anthropology, the themes of Haitian art have represented retentions of African culture in the new world, evidence of survival despite the trauma of the middle passage. But the word discovery here disturbs, just like Columbus "discovered" the new world. The result – the indigenous Taino population was changed forever.

Yet Haiti is, after all this, a land of surprises. In the crevices of the crowded and seemingly anarchic street life of downtown Port au Prince, one finds innumerable well preserved treasures which tell the story of a Haiti past and undoubtedly a presage of a Haitian future. A wizened little old man named Adams Leontus guided me through the Cathedrale Sainte Trinite, reverentially paying his tribute, as he must do with each visitor, to the painters whose works decorate the walls, from floor to ceiling. These are the works of Haiti's grand masters of a so-called primitive or naïve school – Prefete Duffaut, Rigaud Benoit, Castera Bazile, Philome Obin and others. I later realized that he was also one of the accomplished Haitian artists who himself had painted murals for the Cathedral. The themes are biblical, yet reproduced in a Caribbean landscape, populated by Caribbean people. As religion itself has been appropriated and reshaped by Haitian African religion, so too are the images of the saints and the Christian gods, and they are no less inspiring in this place of worship. Perhaps more so - the gods have come home to roost.

At the top of the Rue du Champs de Mars and the scene changes to well tended gardens, a white gleaming palace and impressive statues of the past heroes of revolutionary Haiti These are faultless well-executed pieces of work, impressive to the eye, inspiring to the soul. Perhaps none more so, than the *Marron Inconnu*, the unknown maroon who blew the conch which called the slaves together to action in 1791 in the Bois Caiman. Far more than the European garbed statues of Toussaint L'Ouverture, Henri Christophe, the mulatto Petion and Dessalines, the Marron (as he is referred to fondly by Jean Claude) is alive, the sun beats down on the rough metal as if on his skin,

Lwa – Mixed Media – 12x8 ines – 2015

burnt into a golden black by years of field work. He seems perpetually poised in a call to action, perhaps waiting for a sign once more to sound his shell.

For the duration of our stay at the hotel Montana, meetings continued between the opposition and Lavalas ("flashflood") – Aristide's party, and the Organization of American States, to come to some agreement about the election results to ensure that aid would be forthcoming to Haiti. The deadline for transmission of aid came and went. The dark suited men came and went each day, in large black cars, flanked on each side by armed guards, back and forth, while the colourful tap taps shrugged and heaved with their heavy Haitian load up and down the hills. The dinner conversations over cordon bleu meals continued in Petionville and Kenscoff, about the nature of the Haitian marron personality formed by a history of successful resistance blended with the fatalism of Vodou and Catholicism. In front of the palace and in shouting distance of the statues of *Marron Inconnu* and Toussaint L'Ouverture, a peaceful placard march took place. On Monday morning we were warned not to go downtown, they were burning tires on La Rue Lalue, in front of the immigration office.

The Citadelle at Milot, Cap Haitien, three thousand feet above sea level, stands as a monument to Haiti's will and yet a testament to a perplexing fate and folly. The Citadelle is one of the world's most extraordinary feats of engineering at the time it was built, a fortress of colossal proportions built by Henri Christophe for fifteen years with the labour of over two hundred thousand ex-slaves, twenty thousand of whom died in the process of building it. Christophe was declared President of the State of Haiti in its northern province in 1807 and later named himself King Henri 1 of Haiti, creating a nobility which consisted of four princes, eight dukes, 22 counts and 37 barons, each of whom were given large estates. Although he produced a stable currency still called *gourde* to this day, established a state printing press in the north, created a judicial system known as Code Henri, and saw the education system as pivotal to the advancement of his peoples, he also patterned himself along the lines of the French royalty, building apart from the Citadelle, magnificent castles at Sans Souci, Jean Rabel, Cap Haitien, St. Marc and Petite Riviere. As time went by his megalomania and tyranny increased. His reign has been followed by an almost uninterrupted procession of tyrants and dictators whose sole concern is self-aggrandizement.

We left Haiti with not a little relief, but with a disquieting mixture of sadness, awe and incomprehension of the present historical stalemate in the face of such strength to resist and stamina to survive the centuries of misuse and dictatorships. At the time of writing this, it seemed to me that Haiti has largely become for the Caribbean region an empty shell, once full of sound and fury, now signifying nothing other than that revolution and challenge bring long years of retribution. Haiti does not need our mythologizing or our platitudes, flashfloods followed by long periods of drought. Sustained leadership within and without, committed to helping Haitians liberate themselves from poverty; the political will to compromise when necessary and negotiate the self-defined needs of the majority; treading carefully and righteously and solicitously in the paths once opened by men like Toussaint. These things perhaps could shape a new Haiti.

August 2001

Haiti

Management Cocktail

By Rex Dixon

This hotel is the best in town
The lifts "ne marche pas" neither
                    up nor down
At the weekly cocktails we listen + look
And hear about things not in the guide book
The blonde in tight trousers ain't what
                    she seems
Clinics for sick children is in her schemes
We wonder whether this is a scam
To launder money or ship the damned
She said the lord gather on
                    Oprah Winfrey
We nod and smile and agree
'Cos anything can happen in this
                    town of Hayti

Rex Dixon
Port-au-Prince
4th July 2001.

4th July, 2001

Hotel Montana - Ink on paper - 12x9 ins - 2004

Haiti

Port au Prince Lament

By Rex Dixon

AT THE HÔTEL MONTANA

PORT-AU-PRINCE LAMENT

The men in suits
walk up and down
with bodyguards most black
some brown.
The outside world seems
We haven't a line   far away
the hotel says
The paintings on the street
wont make you weep
walking the pavement
will hurt your feet
The people go on for miles
and miles
I dont know
why they seem
to
smile

Rex Dixon.

5th July, 2001

Outside the Palace – Mixed Media – 9x6 ins – 2004

Australia

Dreaming
down under

Apart from a long delayed promise to see my sister Glenda and her family who were residents in Sydney since the 1980s, maybe it was the self-denigrating humour of the Aussies that drew Rex to agree to this long haul with me. We'd been to a reception at the Australian Embassy in Trinidad some time before and in his welcome speech to the august crowd gathered there the High Commissioner charmed the crowd with his opening joke. "Did you hear the one about the visitor arriving at immigration in Australia? The Officer after going through his travel documents says 'Have you got a criminal record'. Taken aback and nonplussed the visitor responded 'I didn't know I still needed one to enter Australia'".

We journeyed from Trinidad to New York, New York to Los Angeles and then another fourteen hours to Sydney. Thoroughly exhausted after the long haul, I was not in the mood to respect the laws of the land that required the customs officer to search my entire luggage with a fine tooth comb after he found two small sticks of carrot in my handbag – the measly remains of a healthy snack to stave off stomach cramps midflight. Perhaps. I thought to myself, as they searched and searched and found nothing to incriminate me further, they still required a criminal record to enter the country.

But Australia, or at least Sydney and Canberra, was an experience in extremes of art and sophistry of another kind. The landscape and built environments presented unique visual features: from the landmark Opera house to the Sydney Bridge, the stately eucalyptus trees, their bark storing the songlines of generations, to the emphatic aboriginal burial poles that stood like sentries guarding the National Gallery of Australia. The latter were hollow painted poles that contained the bones of the deceased, one of

Sydney Painted Over – Mixed Media – 12x10 ins – 2004

Down Under Dream No 1 – Gouache on paper – 11x7 ins – 2005

Down Under Dream No 2 – Gouache on paper – 11 x 7 ins – 2005

the most moving yet understated cenotaphs that we had seen, accustomed to the mausoleums and stone obelisks of Europe. Everywhere one encountered extremes of friendly helpfulness, except perhaps for the customs official. Yet, in the Victorian sense, a miasma of colonization lingers in the air.

One does not think of Australia without the melancholic awareness of its aboriginal past. It is the country that for some reason has kept alive a most salient memory of the usurpation of land and cultural history in modern times. And perhaps the reason for this is that its aboriginal art has become the signature of Australian creativity, evident in its proliferation among the commercial galleries and main exhibits of the state musea. The one dimensional perspective of painting on canvas exuded movement and deeply incised narratives, as if they were secrets and symbols being passed on to other generations to be decoded. The intricately patterned geographical markings or the stylized emus, birds, lizards and bush laid out on a flat picture plane, evoked a similar manner of filling in space that Rex had identified in early Haitian vodou art.

Apart from photographs and documentaries that we had seen before travelling down under, that sense of loss hauntingly conveyed through various films such as *Walkabout* in 1971 and *Rabbit Proof fence* (2002) had prepared us to be sympathetic onlookers to the aboriginal population. Leaving my sister's household and brood in Baulkham Hills one day to go walkabout in the city of Sydney, it was a strange irony that the first aboriginal man we encountered was drunk and drifting unsteadily on his feet in a central park, as if fulfilling the stereotype of the wasteland that had become the aboriginal mental habitus.

Our visit coincided with the 14th Sydney Biennale in 2004 titled *Reason and Emotion*. A two tonne boulder, huge enough to flatten a small crowd was dropped onto a red car positioned in the front of the Opera house where the exhibition was held. Jimmie Durham's *Still life with Stone and Car* was the centre piece of an exhibition that inside contained room after room of concept oriented sculpture, installation, photographs, performance and one wall of drawings in the style of a child's scrawl, without one painting on view. To take the conceptual legacy of Marcel Duchamp of the urinal fame further, one of the artists given a space in the biennale had auctioned it off to the highest bidder. Rex could not get emotional or involved in the aesthetics of Amilcar Packer's crawl under the carpet or the soft sculpture of off white cushions piled near to the ceiling in the middle of the sofa, or the strewn up

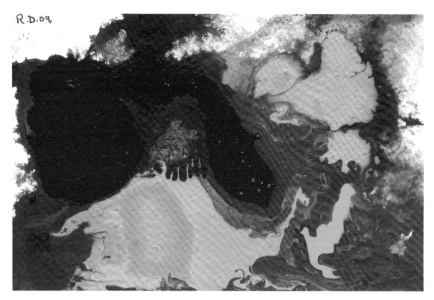

Bent Red – Gouache on paper – 6x4 ins – 2009

objects hidden under the stairwell. Trained in formal art schools in Britain in the sixties when he had struggled to learn how to draw and paint, this iconoclasm and eschewing of traditional formal values of fine art form, subject matter, design and use of colour left him colder than the stone on top of the now immobile red car.

When he came out of the exhibition, the sun was shining on the Sydney Harbour; the boats were dancing jauntily to the sea breeze. He sat down to have a cup of comforting English tea to exorcise the deadening effects of conceptual modernity. And there in front of him, was a black Trinidadian man playing *Waltzing Matilda* on the steel drum, musical tones developed from a discarded industrial object. The magical sounds made from this instrument, drew him back to the remarkable inscriptions of aboriginal signature art first made on the bark of trees and carved in stone. He could not wait to get back to his studio in the green Maracas Valley in Trinidad to begin another painting on canvas.

December, 2015

Sydney, Australia.
Rex Dixon /04

Sydney Australia – Gouache on paper – 11x7 ins – 2005

Escape to Albany

Summer was still in full bloom when we arrived in upstate New York in 2007. The red brick four storey house on upper State Street looked over the lush and welcoming Washington Park. Grey squirrels scampered back and forth burying their nuts in good time for the winter, while the derelicts took advantage of the sun to make full use of the park benches, sipping cheap red wine from bottles hidden in brown packaging, artfully dodging the law.

We moved into a small apartment on the top floor of the red brick, comprising two rooms, a Pullman kitchen and a medium sized bathroom. We had abandoned our sprawling one-acre estate in Trinidad with its bungalow and separate artist studio for the fall semester while I took up a Visiting Professorship at the State University of New York at Albany (SUNY). It was an academic opportunity not to be missed – I would teach two courses, deliver a range of seminars and lectures and get on with my research. Rex was reluctant to leave his studio in the garden in Maracas Valley, in the northern Trinidad tropical hills for this long – just thinking about moving from large canvases to small drawings on paper gave him anticipated withdrawal symptoms. He muttered threats of becoming a conceptual artist. But the separation of over five months was too much for either of us so he relented and agreed to this trip.

I, on the other hand, was eager for a change of academic scenery. I looked forward to working with my colleague Glyne Griffith, in the Latin American and Caribbean Studies Department that had recruited me. I wanted the interaction with a group of gender students drawn from another society to contemplate our own Caribbean gender and sexual differences in

Albany. New York. U.S.A. 24. Nov. 2007

ALBANY NY 122

26 NOV 07PM 2 T

REX DIXON ⋅ PAT MOHAMMED,
5A, MOUNTAIN VIEW,
MARACAS VALLEY.
ST. JOSEPH.
TRINIDAD.
W. INDIES

Albany Postcard No 1 – Mixed Media – 4x6 ins – 2007

the region. I knew at the graduate level I would be teaching students from a range of Latino societies who were attracted to this departmental programme. In addition, the US was such a dominant force in our lives in the Caribbean region and, while my travel and engagements here had been many over three decades, they had been for only short periods for conferences or university meetings, or slightly longer but still abbreviated visiting fellowships at Emory in Atlanta and UC Berkeley, California. Admittedly five months in one university town could not equate to understanding the complexity of this vast society, but I wanted the experience of actually living in the US, carrying out the daily routines of bus rides and grocery shopping, ordering books from Amazon and receiving them by the following day or taking a deluxe train into Grand Central, New York city rather than arriving only by Caribbean Airlines at JFK. When routines become familiar or even mundane, only then do we cross a threshold of learning about a society or even feel a sense of acquaintance.

What I had forgotten, of course, which became the major setback for Rex was the change in seasons over this semester, that summer would turn into autumn and fall into winter. We discovered a cosy pub, which required a lovely walk across the park, and many an evening, arriving with Glyne, I would meet Rex there after work, glasses of draft beer for him, and nicely chilled white wine for us. As autumn set in and the park took on a Persian green with a patterned carpet of crimson and golden leaves, the forays to this pub diminished and by wintertime, it was out of the question.

We tried to get a studio on the campus for Rex to paint and the administration was willing to find him a space. As usual rooms being a premium in any university, this was a kind concession to my spouse. Rex was not impressed with the unused laboratory that was allocated, a good choice for a university given that painters needed sinks and running water and would inevitably drop paint on surfaces. He did not fancy getting into a bus each morning to go to a chilly abandoned lab, especially when at home in Trinidad in his painting shorts and T-shirt, he simply had to venture on to the back porch then to the steps leading down the garden to his studio. Instead, he chose to stay at home in the two room top floor apartment, looking out over Washington square with only the birds and passersby down on the streets as daily contacts. The days that I taught late classes were long, I guess, for him. My schedule on the other hand was full and exciting, Apart from a stimulating graduate class once per week and co-planning a Caribbean seminar with Glyne, I taught an undergraduate class which had two completely different sets of students, one group was black and seemed to come from the poorer sections of Albany, the other was rich, young and Jewish. The early challenges of communication between and among us were whittled away from week to week and, by the end of semester as we sat eating pizzas and drinking Coca Cola to celebrate the last class, I could safely say mutual respect was won all round.

While Rex fulminated about the increasing cold and having to wash in the basement washing machine and bring the clothing up in the diminutive lift to the medium size bathroom to dry, I loved the changing landscape around me, the unbelievable shades of red that autumn brought to the leaves, each like a precious light jewel floating to the ground, or the chill freshness of the morning breeze and the coolness it brought to the cheeks. I reunited with the love I had acquired in Europe for coordinating clothing, selecting a scarf to match the day's ensemble, and the old fashioned personal thermometer

Where to Find Me – Mixed Media – 12x9 ins – 2010

test of sticking a finger out of the window to gage the day's temperature and wind chill factor.

As the weather began to shift however, Rex had located the Amrose Sable Gallery, a small *avant-garde* gallery in Albany owned by Elizabeth Dubben, that loved his work and he had paintings to make. He was due to have an exhibition supported by the Small Axe Collective in September, with pieces we had shipped up to Albany and some he had been working on *in situ*. But clearly Rex had begun to feel rudderless – a Londoner, Ulsterman, Jamaican, Trini situated in the upstate New York with no real purpose. So it was not strange that a section of works in the exhibition were titled "Where to find me" with numerous stamps and arrows as if he was sending smoke signals to the native Americans who had once occupied all of this terrain and to friends from everywhere to rescue him. The only time he cheered up during the pre-exhibition blues was when we went out to dinner with Anthony Winkler, who had been invited to speak at SUNY. Winkler's understated humour transmitted over dinner and in the speech he delivered more than matched that of his fiction.

We enjoyed a few outings together however. One to Boston where anthropologist Diana Fox had urged me over to do a lecture at Bridgewater Community College and we experienced New England hospitality in an American styled well-furnished bed and breakfast establishment on a leafy street in Providence. Another of our New York outings had both ups and downs. Yasser Robles, a student from my graduate class, offered to drive us into New York city as he was heading home to the Bronx for the long weekend. The drive from upstate to the city was definitely pleasing. There were more breathtaking expanses of autumn foliage and, despite the cinematic clichés now familiar with US bridges, a drive over these spectacular inventions was, simply, moving. We booked into an overpriced hotel off Lexington Avenue, very convenient for galleries (Rex and me) and shopping (me only). We spent a glorious weekend, living out snatches of movies, a walk in Central park eyeing the still elusive pull of baseball (to the cricket loving West Indian), or emulating Audrey Hepburn in *Breakfast in Tiffany* and peering at summer displays through Macy's shop windows and had lunch in a Greenwich Village café with Tina and Lee Johnson who lived in Manhattan. The primary purpose of the trip was artistic, to visit galleries and exhibitions MOMA/Frick/Guggenheim/Museo El Barrio and the Jewish Museum. The frothy colours and mannerism of the courting Watteau couples at the Frick were a delight, not far removed from the couples who generously dotted Central Park.

On Sunday, waiting for Yasser to pick us up, a well-stocked flea market set up on pavement and blocked off street left me beside myself with joy. Here was the range of scarves, jewellery and "ethnic" ware that I delighted in. Rex always had a bad reaction to shopping of any sort but his behaviour that morning was more than the usual grumpiness. He said he felt the buildings were leaning in on him on all sides. I could understand this – in comparison to our relatively minute Maracas valley cottage these tall buildings lining both sides of the street, blocking the sunlight, could be intimidating. I was sympathetic to his mood. Heading back to State Street Albany, which in his disturbed state he called "home", it came out that he had had a full cup of black coffee from the dispenser at the hotel. Rex is a classic English tea drinker. A New York coffee was like hard drugs. This traumatic event surfaced in two paintings done on photographs I had taken of New York buildings and, so convincingly did he convey the awesome beauty of the skyscrapers, they sold in Trinidad immediately they were exhibited.

Rex had clearly captured the experience of the small islander in the big city to these avid buyers.

By the end of autumn and moving now into serious single digit temperatures, Rex's mood shifted to an even lower ebb. I threatened to send him home. We compromised, he visited his son Damon in South Carolina for a few days where it was warmer and after an intensive bout of family togetherness with his grandchildren Harley and James, he was happy to rejoin me again. Having experienced the fragility of a ten seater airplane trip to South Carolina he had had enough of flying for a while and had actually missed the Albany space age skyline and the familiar sight of the drunks now huddled in the glass sheltered bus stop, and the excess books at the library, one for a dollar, that we bought and read liberally now that we had more time for reading.

Finally, it was time to leave lovely new friends like Librada Pimental and Patricia Pinheiro that I had made at the department, the free bus pass that took me to SUNY every day, the students who I had prepared for examinations, the little Thai restaurant on Lark Street and the warm basement wine bar we later discovered a stone's throw away from our apartment where Glyne, Rex and I had had many a Yellowtail merlot to ward off the cold. Our return flight had been secured. I started packing up the books and giving them to the second hand bookshop, Rex's unsold paintings were stored or boxed to be shipped, we let the supplies in the fridge dwindle. His mood began to lighten at the thought of his studio space in Maracas Valley again.

By this time, Washington Park had turned into a fairyland at night – the city had erected in neon lights a wonderland of carriages and elves and Santa with his sleigh and reindeer and trains and other wondrous animals along the park. At night cars would drive by slowly to look at the fairy lights exhibition and people would come in droves to simply stare and soak up the magical atmosphere of Christmas. We had the best view, a practically full aerial panorama from our top floor window. Rex remained impassive in the face of all of this glowing radiance. This was no different to his Scrooge attitude to Christmas at home so I left that alone. A few days before we were booked to fly out, it started to snow, not little flakes that fell gently from heaven to the place beneath but large flurry ones that covered everything with about ten eiderdowns of snow. Rex got worried. The news reports began to talk about storm conditions and cancellation of flights. The evening before we were due

Albany Snowed Last Night – Ink on paper – 4x6 ins – 2007

to leave the two old ladies who occupied the first and second floor of the house, invited us over to have some mulled wine and nibbles. We had said hello of course, meeting on the dark red carpeted staircase or exchanging a word here and there about household arrangements, like being informed about the garbage collection when we first arrived. We went over out of duty. Our landlady, an ex-colleague of theirs was someone I knew. She had had a Fulbright with us in St Augustine but she had been on sabbatical out on the west coast so never around. It turned out to be an erudite house as the two old ladies were retired professors – their entire lives spent in the academy – and surrounded by books. It was an enjoyable evening, especially cheerful because of the roaring fire, tasteful Christmas tree and the enchanting crèche centerpiece of the room, a delightful snowy village of Christmas lit objects and animals and figurines decked with artificial greenery. Saying goodnight to them, we regretted not having done this before. They said they wanted to learn more about our lives in the tropics and I would have liked to hear more about their rich academic exploits.

Fairy Tale Snowland – Acrylic on paper – 6x4 ins- 2010

We went up to our top floor and looked out. The snow had stopped falling. There was no sign of a storm. The lights in the park twinkled and shone even more brightly against the pristine white carpet on which they now lay. The snow ploughs would be out by morning to clear a path to the airport. Rex went to sleep at peace with his world. And rising into the air next morning, amidst the engine noise, I thought I heard him say, "It's a pity we couldn't stay longer. I would have liked to get to know those women a bit more". I might have misheard.

January, 2008

India

India

A Coolie's return

When we arrived on the cold Saturday afternoon in January, New Delhi was smothered in a blanket of fog. It had taken me a lifetime to decide on this journey to India. And then we were there and Mother India and mother nature together contrived to keep us circling for another hour above ground. As the pilot finally lowered us onto the tarmac, a dim light twinkled on the horizon of smog. For a brief moment, I imagined this as a departure rather than return, trying to envision the flight of a migrant over a century ago, on a sailboat leaving port, watching her homeland recede into a shadowy distance until all she could see was the feint flicker of a light.

We had come to India to screen the short experimental documentary film *Coolie Pink and Green* at the Pravasi Film Festival, prodded by the Indian High Commissioner in Trinidad, His Excellency Malay Mishra to enter it into the first film festival that celebrated the work of non resident Indians (NRIs) and people like myself, persons of Indian origin (PIOs). For some reason Indians were now interested in what we were making of India from afar. Of my traveling companions and myself only one had been to India before. Sharda Patasar, our musician, had spent four years of a childhood between New Delhi and Agra nineteen years earlier. Rex, my London born husband and co-producer of the film, had perhaps contemplated a trip to India in the sixties as a struggling artist. Michael Mooleedhar, editor of the film, and Christopher Din Chong, co-editor and production assistant, were there to be exposed to another world culture – a generation who had few reference points to anything east of New York. My sensibility was formed from literature, film, history, acquaintances and

Dreaming of India - Gouache on paper - 6x4 inches - 2003

friendships with many Indians from India and of course my own "Indian" experience from Trinidad.

Carole Bagh is a bustling, overpopulated market district, seething with humanity, goods, street vendors, street sleepers, street beggars, street dogs, and street dirt. We crossed the ungainly rubble of construction in the fading light of dusk into the first hotel to which we were ushered, Hotel Vishal. The colours of my film *Coolie Pink and Green* retreated. The fog had lifted to reveal ochres and browns, rust reds and faded olive greens. Dun coloured shawls wrapped Indian style over heads and shoulders and faces and mouths, on ricksha drivers, market vendors and pedestrians, fighting the damp cold of a Delhi winter – we had never seen these scenes on the picturesque screens of Bollywood transported for decades to Trinidad. Besides these, the shops were full of merchandise priced to suit the rupees of a tourist pocket, the scent of Indian assembly lines and factory floors unmistakable – conscience began to immobilize choice.

They say that nothing prepares one for India. That is not quite true. If you have disembarked from a plane in Haiti, you are well prepared for some parts of India. If you have gone to the markets of Katutura in Namibia, you are prepared for some parts of India. If you have seen some of the townships of South Africa or encountered the street children of Brazil you are prepared for India. What *they* cannot describe are the extremes – that one can move from the layers of dirt and effluence of a market street to dinner in a well appointed hotel where *rajput* opulence exudes the pleasures and promise of the legendary eastern sensibility.

The market places were rich and overflowing. Shops selling kurtas, dupattas, hand made leather shoes, some with tips curled like Ali Baba's lamp, intricate woven shawls that took the breath away ranging from the very pricey to the affordable, clothing stalls of women's and men's garments that glittered and shimmered invitingly in the evening light. These contained the employed. There was the layer of the unemployed, the begging classes and castes who seemed to have stepped straight out of Brecht's *Threepenny Opera* and Rohinton Mistry's *A Fine Balance*. The extremes of haves and have-nots, of extravagance and want rubbed shoulders constantly.

We were told that a trip to Agra was a must, despite the shortness of our stay – a 250 mile trip north of New Delhi, made from 6.30 in the morning, traveling through a tunnel of fog for the entire period along a highway that only the seasoned Indian driver could negotiate, weaving around snake charmers and bead sellers, overturned trucks, mourning women, bicycles, *rickshas*, passing villages and small urban settlements that we would only see on our return journey when the fog had lifted. The Taj Mahal in Agra was worth it though. None of the tourist brochures, huge posters, movie shots and picture postcards prepares you for the magnificence of this building. None of the tourist copy came close to describing it for me. When we think of Italy and *amore*, we recall Shakespeare's Romeo and Juliet, inscribed in our literary sensibility as the quintessential tale of tragic love. The Taj Mahal similarly represents India's greatest love story, the monument built by Shah Jehan to his beloved Mumtaz who died in childbirth. Close up, inside the building, its marble and ornate jeweled work are cold and harsh – the beauty lies from afar, and requires that we escape into the creator's intentions. Shah Jehan wanted to look out from his palace window and see Mumtaz in her resting place every day – to imagine her not below the dark surface of earthen ground, rather in an earthly heaven. But she was now of another world. Thus the building rises in middle distance, perfect in its symmetry, a confection of misty lace, echoing of womanhood in the white lingerie-like edges and

Agra Blues – Mixed Media – 7x11 ins – 2010

Crowd at The Taj Mahal – Mixed Media – 7x11 ins – 2010

trimmings, soft rounded globes that temper the pillars and rise up and above, as if floating on a pond in the sky. Each morning for the rest of his life, Shah Jehan must have looked out and imagined her at peace in this white palace in the skies, each dusk, the white marble fading to pink must have added a glow to his memory, each night the luminescent stone and embedded jewels must have sharpened his passion to live and gaze on her another day. This was and is one of the most beautiful testimonies to love that I have seen and a tribute to a civilization that continues to preserve it with care – no one is allowed to walk on the surface without masked covered shoes.

There was little time for shopping or exploration of New Delhi and India, however, as this was a trip with a purpose. *Coolie Pink and Green* had made its debut in Trinidad and had won the award for most popular short local film at the festival in September 2009. The film had gained much attention in Trinidad – the controversial title intrigued; the vibrant colours and music sensuously invited the viewer. But it is a film about cultural disruption, resettlement and conflicts and I was interested in what Indians in India would make of it. I learnt a few weeks before we were to travel to New Delhi that it had been selected by the festival directors to be screened at the opening ceremony of the festival and shown to the huge audience of dignitaries, film buffs, delegates and press who attended openings. The response was overwhelming. Deepa Mehta, the main guest of the opening ceremony and who ignited the flame that began the festival, caught it immediately. "Its visual poetry," she said to me and laughingly followed up with, "So whom did she choose?" the latter in response to the dilemma of the young Indian girl in the film forced by her parents to choose between an arranged marriage and a young man of her own choice of mixed descent. Who wrote the script was a recurrent question; the rhyme and reason for scripting prose and verse resembling the *Ramayana* and *Bhagavad Gita* made sense to this audience used to Sanskrit literature. The collage of old photographs of the early migrants captivated many. This was a surprise. In the Caribbean historians have covered the history of indentureship so thoroughly that it seems redundant for a Trinidad or Caribbean diaspora audience to relive this on film – yet here was an audience of billions for whom this story had yet to be told. A crowd surged around after the screening, reporters followed up with interviews in the *India Times, The Delhi Mail, The Hindustan* and other newspapers, students and scholars interrogated us for the rest of the week of the festival.

Floating SkyWard – Mixed media – 6x8 ins – 2014

I remember one of the first questions that I was asked by an Indian journalist – was this my first trip to India and as a PIO why had I not visited before? India I said, had surrounded me all my lifetime, in its music, cuisine, intellectual achievements, history – as a third generation Trinidadian I could not make a pilgrimage back to a homeland as Trinidad was my home. I could only return when I had something to present India with, the gift of a story of how Indian migrants had transformed India in the Caribbean. A new script was beginning to emerge – *Coolie Pink and Green* was the prequel to a much larger story that needed to be told, a starting point, like a first sentence that remains unfinished in a longer passage I have still to tell.

January 2010

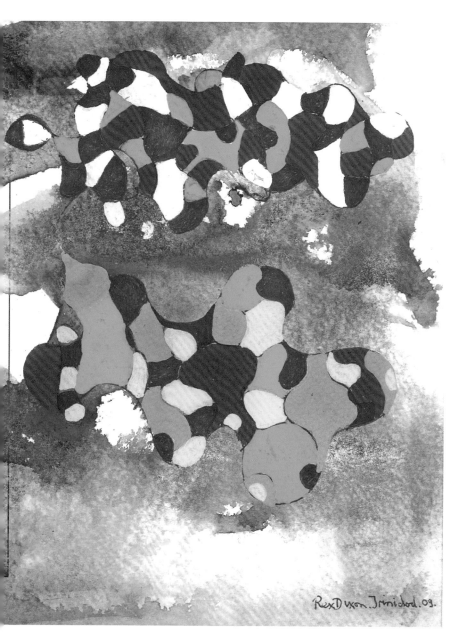

Pink & Green Theme – Mixed Media – 7x12 ins – 2009

Cuba

Cuba

Two men in Havana
(For Graham Gingles)

There is no fictitious secret service or fortunate coincidence in this plot that borrows its title from Graham Greene. But it does deal with the visit of two British men to Cuba in November 2013, and some inadvertent encounters. A visit to Cuba represented an encounter with ideas and ideals. Both men came of age under cold war European politics; one had been a conscientious objector to national army service, the other had lived through IRA besieged Northern Irish history. As artists both were sensible of Cuba's artistic production and one reason for visiting Havana was in fact to better appreciate this artistic outpouring.

Greene's treatment of Havana, popular both as novel and film, did not endear him to Fidel Castro. Greene was primarily poking fun at the British Secret Service but the administration felt he had minimized the terror of Fulgencia Batista's rule. I hope the fidelity and tongue in cheek rendition of the events and experiences of two men in Havana does not suffer the same fate. I am loyal to the idea of the Cuban experiment in socialism, just as I supported the Grenadian revolution in the eighties. Despite their many and various problems, these regimes were attempts to provide alternative governance models for a population.

I have a journalist friend Nazma Muller who had idolized Fidel Castro and the Cuban project of socialism in the Caribbean. She had attempted many times to have an audience with him. This was after he had retreated from public gaze. She eventually succeeded in a personal interview, despite Castro's modus operandi of folding his tents everyday and relocating in a different site each night thus making him a most elusive character. This idea of catching sight of Castro was happily never on our agenda. Rex and another lecturer in his department,

Ernest Hemingway y Fidel Castro .
La Habana 1959
Foto Salas.

CUBA CORREOS 2006
Santa Misa en el Instituto Superior de Cultura Física, Santa Clara
PRIMER ANIV DE LA MUERTE DE JUAN PABLO II
65

3

Rex Dixon & Pat Mohammed
3A. MOUNTAIN VIEW
MARACAS VALLEY
ST · JOSEPH
TRINIDAD & TOBAGO
W. INDIES

La Habana Postcard – Mixed Media – 4x6 ins – 2008

Cecil Cooper had taken students from the Jamaican Edna Manley School for Visual Arts on a field trip in the early 1980s to look at the Cuban art, and had visited the art school, which was the former country club for the old Baptista regime. Funnily enough Baptista himself was not allowed in the same club as he was black. They had stayed in the Hotel Inglaterra in Old Havana. Rex had stories of and recalls the shortages that locals experienced while the tourist dollar could purchase scarce goods, and being solicited to buy cigars on the balcony of the hotel.

This visit with Rex and Graham was my third to Cuba and I still had not had the opportunity to venture further afield than Havana, its compelling, enigmatic main city that reminds me of a beautiful señora whose finest features are obscured by a tattered mantilla. In 2008, Rex had then accompanied me to another conference at the University of Havana. He was as usual interested in the museums and art galleries, the street art and music, the tall tales of Ernest Hemingway. He had lived through the Bay of Pigs episode of the 1960s and still retracts with horror at the memory of this moment when the world seemed on the brink of a third conclusive world war.

No Muchas Gracias Señora – Gouache on paper – 12x9 ins – 2013

Small Hotel Telegrafo Cuba No 1 – Ink on paper – 12x9 ins – 2013

Street Encounter – Gouache on paper – 11x12 ins – 1996

We stayed at the Hotel Nacional, then with its impressive old colonial architecture, checkerboard black and white floors, turrets and arched entrances, grandly looking out over the Malecon on one side and the majestic driveway to the city streets on the other.

This, our latest trip to Cuba was in 2013. It was Graham Gingles's first, a birthday present from Rex and myself on one of his visits to the West Indies.

Graham and Rex are two very different looking characters; Rex is tall and slender with a still full head of white hair, or strawberry blonde, as he was once called by a hopeful customer in a gay bar in The Netherlands. Rex is impassive and unapproachable to the onlooker, a version of the stiff upper lip lurking somewhere in his genes, surfacing quickly if a stranger tries to engage him. Graham is shorter, with a cuddly figure and a very expressive face, an open curious look with eyes that are constantly taking in the activities around him. It is no wonder then that both had completely different experiences in Havana, although one must say that some of this was circumstantial.

Rex had been coming down with the flu' from the time we set out from Trinidad. So most of his time in Havana on this visit was spent in the expansively sized room in the Hotel Telegrafo, his rest interrupted by the repetitive chorus made by the touts selling taxi services outside of the hotel room. He roused himself up sufficiently to make the pilgrimage to the Museo Nacional de Bellas Artes de La Habana, an impressive collection that predates the colonial era and establishes the ground breaking traditions in Caribbean art movements. But Graham and I alone ventured forth to walk the streets, and lunch in the sidewalk restaurants, to visit one after the other atelier of Cuban artists. This was the daytime events that Graham and I shared. Graham is nocturnal in his habits however and liked the freedom of the night walking the streets, finding bars to listen to live Cuban bands and singers. And invariably he was solicited by beautiful senoritas of the night. Graham was flattered by this unusual attention, pondering that the several approaches to his person would provide much food for dinnertime conversation when he returned to the cold winters in Northern Ireland.

Being gender sensitive, I asked him on the flight back through Panama whether he had found out the price for such services. But a shy and restrained Irishman in strange circumstances, he had acquainted himself with the unconventional response "No muchas gracias señora", thus leaving both parties with their dignity fully intact.

December, 2013

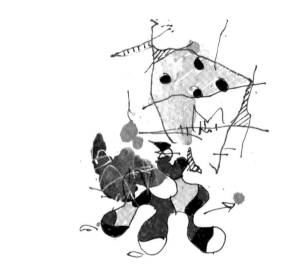

Barbados

Barbados

Fifty shades of blue

Taxi drivers are a fount of information in any country and Barbados has some of the nicest taxi drivers we have yet to encounter. As they drive you to your hotel they can tell you about the rich and famous that they chauffeur to the elite and secluded high priced hideaways that this country is famous for, about the political climate of the day, who is in favour and who is out, who is batting or winning in the current cricket match and where to find the best places to eat and drink. They humour your yearning for freshly caught and cooked fish like that served in Oistins and Baxter's road, although friends Andy Taitt and Kamala Kempadoo did recently introduce us to a good alternative on the west coast road. We don't want to hazard a guess as to why the fish in Barbados tastes so good, but we swear it has something to do with the blueness of the sea. After leaving the olive through murky greens of the waters that one encounters around Trinidad, with the exception of Tobago's Nylon Pool and the teal sparkle of a sunny Maracas Bay on its north coast, there is nothing that compares with the aquamarine feast of the Barbados western coastline, which effortlessly seduces the eye on a sunny day.

Barbados was the first island that I ever visited in the Caribbean several decades ago. The red post boxes and the Barbadian burr had a similar cadence to west of England that I would only later connect. This retention of an English heritage is no longer fiercely regarded but the remnants of undulating pastoral landscape outside of the more populated urban areas, the royal palms that lined plantations, the conical stone structures that survived from sugarcane windmill factories, the vernacular British architecture and diminutive chattel houses that typify older buildings, are constant reminders of this troubled history.

Bus Ride– Gouache on paper – 3x8 ins – 2010

Many of my visits are spent on The University of the West Indies, Cave Hill campus, the location an enviable one. Situated on a plateau as one rises the hill, the campus overlooks a view of the sea in the near distance. Its central focus is the superb arc of cricket pitch, pavilion and stands, built under the administration of Principal Sir Hilary Beckles, an eloquent repossession of a game and tradition that once was the claim of the empire. One sits in meetings on the top floor of the Akan Stool, the relatively newly constructed Administration building of this campus, and while we solve the concerns of knowledge delivery, the sea glimmers, glistens and beckons in the distance, an unperturbed and timeless blue.

Rex has not travelled on the many trips that I make into Barbados as these are primarily work related and short term. However, he has been with me there for research purposes and for several conferences, one of which was held on the Atlantic coast near Bathsheba, a different mood of Barbados, which for him resembled the Cornwall that he lived in during the sixties. Domiciled for years in the Caribbean, Rex who stands out because of his skin colour, does not make a good tourist in these islands. Often treated as a tourist, sometimes addressed with a pseudo North American drawl and solicited to buy souvenirs on the beach, does not appeal to his sense of identity.

However some friends of ours from Northern Ireland, Robert and Fiona Gingles did enjoy the touristic pleasures when they flew in to Barbados to go sailing on the world championships for GP14 dinghies. When not on the high or low seas they took one of the tours given by a young man who carries out a class act served with rum punch all the way including, as Fiona told the story, when they passed a building with an old woman he tells the passengers of the day, "Say hello to Aunty Betty". His transmission of island domesticity,

a well organized itinerary and his comic standup routine with fellow guides makes this tour both professionally run as well as having its unique "bajan" flavor. For a country that is heavily dependent on tourism, Barbados has not represented for both Rex and myself a tourist destination. Rather it has been a space that is an extension of Caribbean regionality, producing its own cultural branding and thus for us a constant exploration of its artists among many others, Ras Akyem Ramsay and Ras Ishi Butcher, writers George Lamming and Kamau Braithwaite, cricketers Sir Garfield Sobers and Wesley Hall, singers The Mighty Gabby and Alison Hines, and scholarly friendships especially that of Eudine Barriteau, Philip Nanton and Jane Bryce.

Barbados Surf – Acrylic on paper – 3x9 ins – 2015

Next to the island of Jamaica, Barbados has become the familiar and family island in the region. Each time I arrive in Barbados I am lulled into a sense of order, real or imagined, that characterizes the land and its peoples. And each time, flying out of Barbados, as the plane ascends just above the shoreline and the coral reefs, that sense of an ordered landscape from above is encrypted, like textured stone set in a jeweled ocean that contains fifty shades of blue.

February, 2016

Northern
Ireland

Northern Ireland

Surviving Belfast
By Rex Dixon

When I arrived in Belfast in 1981 the City Centre was barricaded off, buses were combed by security guards for explosives, and everyone was searched before entering shops. Armed British soldiers patrolled the streets. There was graffiti everywhere, with Protestant and Catholic areas easily found by their markings. Not a restaurant was open at night. The streets were deserted. Luckily I had found somewhere to live at Bonney Before just outside Carrickfergus, north of Belfast. It was a *one up one down* terraced cottage within yards of Belfast Lough, very basic with the *loo* in the garden at the back. It was all I could afford. I was trying to support a mortgage on a house near Birmingham – being a one-parent family with a troubled teenage son installed in that house.

Looking for work as a lecturer in painting in Margaret Thatcher's Britain was not easy. I had got a short-term contract teaching painting on the B.A. Course in Fine Arts at what was then called the Ulster Polytechnic, now the New University of Ulster in Belfast. The students were energetic and hard working in an environment that was falling apart around them. Bomb scares were frequent and when these occurred we had to vacate the building to McGlades bar across the road to continue tutorials over a pint, not the greatest of hardships whilst the bar remained standing. Every so often someone was sent to telephone the college to see if the all clear had been sounded, calling from the public telephone in those pre-cellular days. "No, no," we would be warned, "its not an all clear yet." So you stayed put. The bar was on the first floor with no windows, so you never knew if it was day or night. If you had the extra pint and missed the last train to Larne, you had to get a taxi. Unless of course Graham Gingles, an artist whom I had met at gallery openings

Two Burning Cages – Acrylic on canvas – 57x40 ins – 2013

in Belfast who patronized the bar from time to time, was drinking at McGlades, and he would give me a lift and drop me off at Downshire on his way up to Ballygalley. Most of the time, however, I would have to brave the taxi office that was quite near to the Divis flats, a Republican stronghold. When you walked from McGlades bar to find a taxi, army helicopters would fly over continually lighting up the streets with their searchlights, a very macabre scenario. It was surreal – like the blitz, with the whirring sound of the helicopter engines above and the sharp focused lighting moving back and forth across the dimly lit streets. You knew you were being observed and even listened to all the time. The taxi office was a small box room with a grilled microphone through which you communicated your destination. You never

saw the hidden operator. In those troubled times, my London accent would mark me out for what I was, a Brit. The British army was an occupying force in Northern Ireland as a further extension of the Troubles which had been going on for several decades, if not centuries. The IRA was bombing Britain and Northern Ireland. There was a civil war within Ulster. There were informers everywhere. They must have got it right that I was not a member of the armed forces or an undercover informant, because I am still here to tell this tale.

I had no bathroom or studio so I used to get to work early to shower and painted in a windowless storeroom at the College. I managed nonetheless to produce sufficient work and had several shows in Belfast while I lectured at

Beyond the Hills – Ink on paper – 6x20 ins – 1990

Ulster, including one at the Arts Council Gallery, a buildings that subsequently was blown up. The three-year contract that I had in Belfast expired and I was back on the dole in England in 1984. Sitting in the local library trying to keep warm one day I saw three painting jobs advertised in the international section of the *Times Educational Supplement*. They were in Jamaica, Nigeria and Tasmania. I said to myself I will apply for all three and the first one that comes up "me gone". It turned out to be Jamaica and that's where nine years later Pat and I met when she arrived fresh from The Netherlands to take up a teaching post at the University of the West Indies in Kingston.

May, 2016

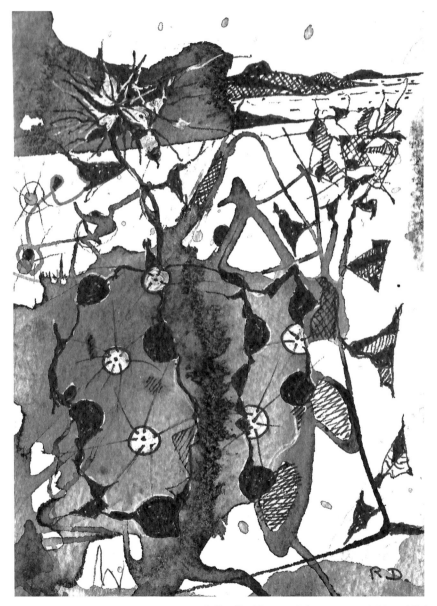

Ballygalley Flowers – Ink on paper – 6x4 ins – 2014

Northern Ireland

Poems written by
the Light of the Irish Sea
(For Graham Gingles)

1. Ballygalley sur la mer

The ivy's climbed on the front cottage wall
Things grow so much in spring
The hollyhocks I planted last summer
now blooming purple and pink
The garden's overrun with five cats, next door
Tara bearing brownies on a plate with a glowing smile,
"Welcome back", she says, "you've brought the weather
with you".

Its quiet tonight
The first deep sleep for months,
Dreaming of books to write
With titles like pink hued blues,
the tint of the sky last night at eleven o'clock
when only the waves were awake

Rex rousing me with half an Irish breakfast
"Lough's will be proud of me," he declares.
We've both come home to rest.

2. Village walk on a cloudy day

High, high above
A grey cotton cloud smothers Larne
Stealing Cairncastle Hill and the Mull of Kintyre across the sea swell
The horizon has vanished, the village is under a spell

An eerie quiet reigns until one can hear
the drone of far approaching cars
and the playful slip slapping of the brook
sloshing under the bridge
the ambient sound track of a film.
White cottages trimmed with green
Lie side by side in flattened repose,
No shadows, movement, not even a sunlight glint
to cheer the flowers with a glow.

I return just in time to listen
to rain against the conservatory roof
tap tapping to get in.
And in the garden, the orange nasturtiums
curtsey,
Then lift their heads to drink.

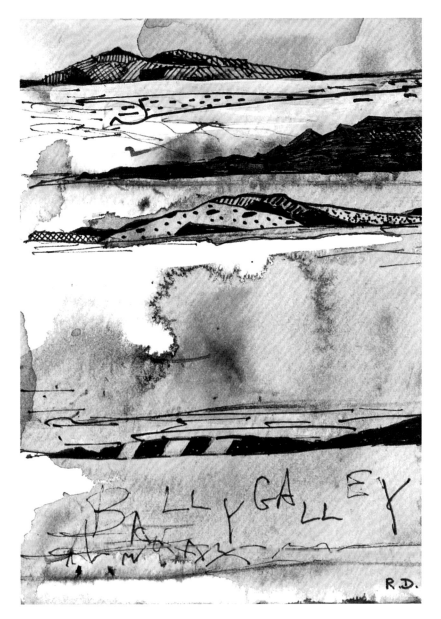

Ballygalley No 1 – Ink on paper – 6x4 ins – 2014

Ballygalley No 2 – Ink on paper – 6x4 ins – 2014

3. The Shambles light at evening's flight

The lazy sunlight drifts alongside
patches of people dotting the lawn
moving as they are, with the evening rays
to catch the fading warmth.

Hillsboro a twee part of the island
where Queenie has one of her residences
and visits once or twice per year
to keep her hand in the Irish till.

Sunshine mutes the cold that seeps
into tropical fingers, ankles and toes.
Toby's four children run back and forth
making children's noises
keeping the air fresh and blended
with the smell of barbecued hamburger and sausage.
"The classic American hotdog," says the chef
topping up with ketchup, mustard and smoked onions.
The evening tastes washed down with chardonnay.

And beautiful young blondes
Stroll hand in hand with Beckham like young men,
Bare armed, and tight trousered legs flashing summer freedom.
The indoor antique furniture, bronze sculpture and paintings
take second place to life and living.
And old artists' eyes record the light
From fading gold, to clover, to musty dark.
Will Alan sell any wooden coffins today?

August, 2012

Evening Light – Gouache on paper – 6x4 ins – 2014

4. On to Mattie's Meeting House

The two mile walk a mere Sunday evening stroll
past Croft Road, down Hidden Dip
slowly climbing up the hill
Half a dry cider and a Guinness for you
Sparkling amber, liquid jewel in a glass
and dark velvet with a foaming white cap,
The finest day yet, the patio is filled with Irish folk
enjoying a pint or two
"Hello Charlie boy, what yer doin here," one says to a
red haired lad.
"We're in for a feed"
"We're in for a feed, too" they say, "where's your da?"
As Charlie's father leaves his clan and joins them in a round
Enjoying the craic they were, male laughter ringing out
A happy sound in Mattie's meeting house

Baa says the sheep next door
Competing with the men
Farmyard music fills the air
The conversation flows
Bleating sheep and mooing cows
And farmhands shouting yay yay
The waiter comes out and adds his bit
"Watch out for them boys with the wellies on
running after the sheep."
"Well you might get an ugly one."
And the craic continues
As the evening beats down in Mattie's meeting house.

Parade (Ballygalley) – Mixed Media – 12x9 ins – 2008

Northern Ireland

Halfway House Hotel
(for Jude Stephens)

There is a pub on the Antrim coast
It's called the Halfway House
Its been the site of many a good meal
And Lord I know I've supped.

Dear Peter the wolf has served us well
An extra chip he said
You looked like you needed a rare good feed
adding enough champ to fill a bed.

The last heron just dipped for a fish
In the marinated blue grey bay
The conversation drifts back and forth
As Jude joins in to say
Graham is this your last dessert
Before the diet starts,
Oh yes, he quips
Can't you see,
That I just refused a tart.

The tide is high, the pub light dims
The evening's drawing on
The summer solstice a wondrous sight
But we must relieve the sun.

June 2014

Couple – Ink on paper – 8x11 ins – 2008

Northern Ireland

Lilies across the valley
(For Zuleikha Mohammed and Edna Betty Dixon)

My mother would have loved this walk
The daisies scattered like yellow dots on green
She would have stopped at each wild flowering shrub
Rifling plants for her front yard,
And, arriving at the crossroad on the hill
looked down at the receding dale
And upwards to the pub that lay ahead.

Zuleikha would have savoured the smells of this summer's day
Responded 'not me' coyly to a glass of chilled white wine
Considering it, as she drew a cooling sip,
as refreshing water, liberated from the vine.

In the pub garden lies a large wooden crate
filled with blush red star lilies,
unfolding from their leafy growth,
still in time to catch the last of the summer warmth

We ordered white lilies for Edna's box
their beauty too quickly stemmed as the heat unfurled.

My mother's smile so close, yet far away
like valleys crossed and gone, and gone to stay.

July 2015

Flowers in a Boat – Ink on paper – 8x6 ins – 2014

Northern Ireland

On thinking about buying a cottage on the Antrim coast

Extricated from the computer for a walk to a house
while sneaking a last look at Jamie Oliver's fifteen minute meals
mouthwatering television viewing
A wodge of this and a waz of that he says
Tastefully filling even the rainy days.
The snot green sea today with swathes of clever blue
under a classic summer sky
The sun shining as bright as a button in my eye
But a treacherous breeze blowing across the water
separating the sheep from Patsy
who has dreams of buying a cottage here
bold face bold face viewing the pricey two bedroom detached,
perched on a hillside in Ballygalley.
Irish coastline on the east
and the glacier smooth hills of Cairncastle on the west
A place where the sea and land, both hold my hand.

July 2015

Downshire No 1 – Ink on paper – 5x12 ins– 1990

Trinidad
Again

Trinidad

Its always
a quarter past twelve

A half past crawl through Valencia, the fat lady setting out her goods
Cowheel soup today, her pot as big as the moon.
Salybia Bay is at rest, waters reflecting the muddy silk-cotton clouds above
Only the road works moving in this midday heat.

We arrive at Balandra cottage by the sea,
the grass has grown greener,
Sky falls on Blue house,
as calmly as the breeze that never reaches its sheltered porch,
Today is hollow and still.

Park the electric blue car, darn that dream,
Take one, Thelonius Monk alone and us
Un-tracking, unpacking
Blue igloo for hibernation,
Camera, computer, two bags of books,
Pencils and a sketch pad or two,
Forgot the underwear, who cares
The clock on the bedroom wall is always a quarter past twelve.

July, 2009

Balandra Drawing - Pencil on paper - 12x16 ins - 2009

Trinidad

Beach walk
in the morning

Last night the moon and clouds played hide and seek,
Below them, a glassy sea appearing and disappearing in their game.
Come and see this, you say, look at the dark outlines against white.
The Canon shutter speed slows down to a halt, a pause
to absorb diffused silver light
Until the rain drives us in doors again.

This morning the beach is fresh and wide and open handed.
Zorba's feet on a stretch of sand,
Jackson Pollock eat your heart out rocks,
Brancusi sculpture in perfect miniature symmetry,
A beautiful boy balancing on his surfboard, waiting for curvy waves,
The sea is kind today.

July, 2009

Toco Moods – Acrylic and collage on paper – 9x12 ins – 2010

Trinidad

Arthur's Rest and Bar
(For Rex)

Holed up at the beach house for five days on end
Not a body passes by
For company Patsy on the computer, some books and myself
Just the right distance from the sea spray but absorbing the sand
We run out of drinks and food and feel for the taste of someone else's hand

Arthur's restaurant and bar in Rampanalgas, two miles up the road
Four Stag, one soda, two tonic water and one coke
Two bikers drive up in roadsters larger than Neil's
Middle age crisis writ large on their heels
They head for the bar, order two Carib, if you pleeze
And then proceed to drink and shoot the breeze
One rasta in a tam, another clean t-shirt dude,
and two young boys from the village, looking longingly at the food.

Just in time for early lunch, we order from Mrs. A,
Chatty type while dishing out souse and callaloo
She notice Patsy taking pictures of yours truly and say she jealous,
and you want more pepper in the food?
A body builder with biceps and shoulder larger than the Yaris
With two ample women, like one not enough for him.
Cars and SUV's drive up and find place to park
Middle age types with younger women in tow
Spilling out from vehicles, coming in for so

Studio Dreaming – Mixed Media – 8x12 ins – 2011

Exhaust from trucks passing, a Honda in the parking lot blasting a tune
The bird in the bird cage stop trying to whistle, and swoon
Can't even get near the lyrics, the noise level is hell
Its time to leave and get back to my cell.

July, 2009

Trinidad

Goodbye John,
Hello Dolly

J ohn was not a handsome man, far from it. He had a prominent pockmarked proboscis that dominated his face and a toothy smile that because of the many gaps was more menacing than welcoming. But he was a true son of the soil and a relic of ancient time past in the Maracas valley where we settled after leaving Jamaica in 2002.

He came to work with us as a gardener. I am not even sure how we found him, or he found us. Rex thinks the plumber with the bad leg who had his toes cut off sent him. When John arrived at work in the morning, he changed from relatively unfashionable but respectable clothes to threadbare trousers held at the waist with rope and zipped up with safety pins, and a denim shirt that had been patched and re-patched until the original seams were lost. But John on Saturdays, lower down the main road in the village where he lived, became quite Jack the lad, white trousers, blue double breasted blazer, large dark shades covering much of the nose and a cap like one worn by merchant captains, looking for all the world like a millionaire (not a little reminiscent of *Some like it hot*). He was your equal.

The sprawling white and blue wooden bungalow and a separate two storey studio for Rex in the same colonial style house and garden on an acre of lush forest land where weeds and tropical wild life could take over in a blink, were a tad bit over what we could manage without help. So we recruited John and, just before him, Girlsin as the household helper and together they were a two days a week fixture for over a decade. Girlsin was short and pleasantly plump, with dark hair, a ready smile and very even tempered. Although she came to us as a cleaner, very soon we realized that Girlsin's forte was not with the broom and the bucket but with the pot and

Maracas Valley House – Mixed Media – 11x 8 ins – 2016

spoon. She was an excellent cook. In somewhat typical Trinidadian style, we feed everyone who comes by or works for us and we realized one day that we had more accidental visitors on the days Girlsin worked than on others.

The St Joseph River forms one of the boundaries of our property and criss crosses at various places the single roadway into the hills of Maracas Valley. This same river had brought Spanish soldiers up from the Gulf of Paria into the interior to erect the city of St Joseph, the first capital city of Trinidad for 300 years. Much of our history of the valley however was gleaned not from history books but from John's storehouse of reminiscences. The entire Mountain View community in which we lived was once a tonka bean estate owned by a French Creole land owning family. Heavy, half submerged slabs of aging concrete on our back slope were the remains of the drying house. Rex's studio site in the back garden once housed the horses that pulled the estate carts. The horseshoes we unearthed when the foundations of the studio were being laid, confirmed John's reminiscences.

Today our land is a mature fruit and flower garden with iguanas, birds, bats and lizards, the occasional snake washed up by the river, agouti and manicou and countless frogs and mosquitos. John looked after the Julie mangoes, sapodillas, guavas, oranges, otaheite apples, bananas, limes and avocados. He tended the anthurium beds and the numerous plants that I constantly introduced in pots and beds and hanging baskets. He arrived promptly at eight in the morning and we would make him his cup of tea and he and Girlsin would catch their breaths from walking up the hill to our house and gossip about the daily news of Trinidad gleaned from the newspaper and radio. Neither of them had ever set foot outside of Trinidad, not even to Tobago.

They were very protective of both of us. One day when I was out of the country Rex had to leave very early on an errand. John had come in earlier and was working at the back of the house, so Rex thought it was safe to leave the front door slightly ajar for when Girlsin arrived. She walked into the house and a strange man appeared in the bedroom door. Her first thought was a workman doing some odd job but some suspicion forced her to question him and she asked, "Where Mr. Rex?" "Down at the bottom of the garden" the man replied. Now Girlsin was not born yesterday. The car was missing so she hotfooted - not her usual pace - out to where Mr. John (as she always called him) was hacking at weeds. "Where Mr. Rex", she asked. "It have a man in the house". Well John needed no further bidding. Cutlass

Maracas Valley Studio – Mixed Media – 11x8 ins – 2016

in hand he sprinted in his wellington boots up to the house, making for the bedroom where Girlsin had seen the man. By this time the bird had flown, leaving evidence of his ransacking. Their intervention was timely and he got away only with packets of foreign currency, notes left over from trips, some valueless and could not be changed in Trinidad and that I held on to for comparative visual iconography of currency, a project I never resuscitated. When Rex returned they were both seated in the front of the house, John still clutching the cutlass, ready to come to our rescue if the man showed up again. Not much gardening or cooking was done that day, with the police called in and the incident relived again and again.

John and Girlsin were protective also of our spiritual welfare. Another day I brought home a Shiva Lingam, a decorative ceramic shape with snake's head, a symbol of Lord Shiva that is venerated by Hindus as representative of creation. Consistent with Hindu practices I placed it in my garden, among a rockery affair just outside the back windows. Moving around the house I kept hearing a *sub voce* discussion on the back step between John and Girlsin, and peeping out, I could see much gesticulation and emphasis between them. Then Girlsin came into the house quietly and approached me in the study. "Miss Patsy, Mr. John say that you cyar put the Shiva outside your bedroom window". "Why not", I asked in real surprise. "Because Lord Shiva could see you when you changing your clothes and they say that must not happen. And too besides, the sun must rise and set on it," Girlsin replied seriously. "But Mr. John is a Catholic, what he know about this? You are Hindu, this is true?" I retorted astounded. My introduction of the stone figure as decoration was clearly not sufficiently appreciative of its value to devotees. "Yes, I agree with him" Girlsin said in her non-confrontational way. "It will bring bad luck to the house." Rex and I discussed this household conundrum. It looks nice on the rockery, Rex mused. But they said that we will have bad luck if we leave it there, and I don't want to offend them, really, I pondered aloud. So without any fanfare the Shiva lingam was unobtrusively moved that day to the front of the house, far far away from any accidental glimpses of naked flesh. The sun continued to rise and set on it for years before the elements finally cracked it open.

John and Girlsin settled back happily into their routines for another decade, caring for the house on our trips, and greeting us with a vase full of red and pink anthurium lilies when we returned from sojourns abroad. Nothing lasts and they aged along with both of us, with different ailments. One day John had to stop working. It had become increasingly difficult for him to

bend over the garden beds and although he continued to put in his full eight-hour day without fail, it was clear that he needed to slow down. We said good-bye to him regretfully and reluctantly, this gentleman of the soil who belonged to the valley. We heard that he was ailing, and visited him, and sometime later his family informed us that he had died. We went to his funeral service in the two hundred year old Roman Catholic Church in St Joseph and thought it fitting that John was buried in the nearby cemetery, in the village where he had worked for over sixty years.

Mr. Oliver succeeded Mr. John. He and Girlsin struck up a good acquaintance after some initial loyalty to John on Girlsin's part. But, soon after, Girlsin's health began to give way and she also had to leave. Mr. Oliver is more stockily built and at least twenty years younger than John. Mr. Oliver established a nice routine, a cup of tea first thing in the morning made by Rex, a little light work from 9 to 12, lunch courtesy the employers, siesta right after lunch in the store room which he converted into a makeshift bedroom with a discarded large cardboard box that he lays out as a bed. He makes up rap lyrics while he works and sings tunelessly and happily as a sand boy as he waters the garden and moves things around with a wheelbarrow.

Without Girlsin the house started to look dishevelled even though she had not ever managed to clean or dust anything above her eye level, roughly four feet five inches. But we suffered more from the withdrawal of her wonderful home cooked hot meals at least twice per week, although Rex's beans on toast were a tasty substitute. Mr. Oliver came to the rescue, cajoling a younger woman away from another household in the neighbourhood to try her luck with us. I told Rex one day that we were to have another helper. Fine he said, I hope she can clean better than she can cook he said, looking at the dust particles rising thickly around us in the early morning light. We can try her out I said. She came over and interviewed me one day to see if she was trading one unhappy situation for another and seemed satisfied enough with what she saw to agree that she would work for us. I liked her immediately, young, good looking, cheerful and intelligent, the last two especially treasured in any employee. The morning she was due to start working with us, Rex thought for the first time to ask me her name. I told him. He smiled gleefully. He insisted on getting up that day bright and early to open the door for her so he could greet her with the classic movie line. "Hello Dolly" he said as he ushered her in, "welcome to our home".

January, 2016

Mr John's Funeral – Acrylic on canvas – 57x40 ins – 2013

Previous versions publication acknowledgments

"Uneventful days in Mayaro", "A Coolie's return", "A World on a little hill" and "Mi dawta, mi dawta" were published in various newspapers or magazines.

"The Fisherman of Flagaman and other tales of a treasured beach" was published in *Sunday Guardian Newspaper*, Trinidad and Tobago, January 24, 1999

"Haiti, I'm Sorry" was published in *Trinidad Express*, Thursday July 12, 2001.

"Cricket watching and other voyeuristic sports" was published in *Postmarks from Paradise: The Philatelic & Numismatic History of West Indies Cricket* by Albert W.B Sydney, Sydney House, Port of Spain, 2010.

Note to readers

Unless otherwise acknowledged as Rex Dixon's prose or verse, the text was authored by Patricia Mohammed.